Newsvesting

Newsvesting

Use News and Opinion to Grow Your Personal Wealth

MATT TOWERY

LOOKING GLASS BOOKS

Published by
Looking Glass Books, Inc.
Decatur, Georgia

Distributed by John Blair, Publisher
Winston-Salem, North Carolina

Copyright © 2015 Matt Towery

ISBN 978-1929619610

Book and cover design by Burtch Hunter Design
Manufactured in the United States

Acknowledgments

I want to acknowledge numerous individuals who helped me in becoming a Newsvestor and in writing *Newsvesting*.

I want to thank Mac McGrew and his team at the Harrison McGrew Group at Morgan Stanley. Mac and I have worked together for many years in many roles. While he is a professional investment advisor and I am not, we have learned Newsvesting together. He and his team are the best.

I certainly want to thank my two collaborators, Bill Lewis and Gary Reese, for their fine research, editing, and wordsmith. Both are true professionals.

Thanks goes to Matthew Towery, Jr. Matt has taken the opinion research I once headed at InsiderAdvantage to a new level of sophistication with his research firm Opinion Savvy.

Additional thanks to Dick Parker at Looking Glass Books and his brilliant designer Burtch Hunter.

I also want to express my sincere appreciation to my colleagues at InsiderAdvantage including Phil Kent, Patrick Hickey, and Louie Hunter. Also much thanks to the editors and staff at Creators Syndicate as well as everyone at my law firm of Hall Booth Smith, PC. Also much thanks to my colleagues at FOX5 Atlanta.

My mentor and friend Newt Gingrich gave me valuable input and encouragement. We have worked together for decades and his support as always was tremendous.

And most of all I want to thank my best "editor," friend, and wife, Dolle Eckert Towery. Without her this book would never have happened. It is to her this book is dedicated.

Contents

How to Make Money Using the Computer Between Your Ears
(With a Little Help from Your Gut)

Here's a simple question: Do you want to make money? Legally, of course. Seems silly to ask, right? Everybody wants to make money. But here's another simple question (or two): Would you like to build your own personal wealth or at the very least hold on to what you have by monitoring the forces that most impact the corporate entities that make up our publicly traded markets? Or do you want to listen to what everyone else says you should do?

After all, everyone knows that you should avoid letting headlines or public opinion surveys drive your investment strategy, right? Well, maybe not.

Imagine if you were heavily invested in the housing market or in the banks that were flourishing as a result of that market in early 2006. Suppose you had mortgaged your home and used the cash to invest in the stock market or a small business idea that you wanted to make a reality. If given a lead time while homes were still selling and prices were still strong, would you have moved to get out before the bottom fell out in the housing market? Would you have unloaded those bank stocks? Mostly likely, yes.

Let's say it's early 2008. The stock market was still strong and the presidential campaign was dominated by issues such as ending the war in Iraq and how to deal with undocumented or illegal aliens. In the midst of all this, you heard that a major investment vehicle used by the big investment firms on Wall Street had started to fail. Would you have taken it as a signal that an economic meltdown would rear its ugly head some six months later? Would you have made the appropriate changes to help save your 401(k) or your private investments? Again the answer is likely yes.

Certainly many experts on Wall Street and indeed many sophisticated investors around the world would concur that relying on news events to determine how, when, or where to put your money not only doesn't work but can be extremely dangerous.

Well, not every expert. In recent years many companies have started to use or offer to the public software that uses so-called *algorithmic trading*. These algorithms account for a set of variables in securities trading. A search for stock-market prediction models can easily lead an investor to scores of software-based or online systems that provide real-time predictive assistance for not only U.S. stocks but foreign markets, currency exchanges, and commodities such as gold.

More recently news stories and social media have been incorporated into the mix of variables used by several organizations and their software. Often these systems are used in what is known as *high-frequency trading*.

But the best of these systems, for the most part, are unavailable to average investors, except in the sense that their financial managers might rely on them on their clients' behalf. While some of these algorithm-driven systems boast good if not great results, the truth is that most investors are scared enough just trying to choose a stock, a mutual fund, or an ETF, much less select which computer-based analytical system could potentially lead them toward financial success in publicly traded markets.

And, of course, the idea of capturing rapidly shifting stock prices through software or an online site seemingly suggests a now dirty word: day trading.

In its simplest form, day trading involves buying and selling securities on the same trading day. When the tech bubble burst in 2000, far too many inexperienced and undercapitalized day traders were wiped out. Their daily routine of booking profits on small movements in the market—whether buying and selling equities or playing in the more sophisticated and dangerous futures market—became a nightmare. The term *day trading* immediately assumed a pejorative nature, suggesting greed and stupidity, a kind of financial gambling.

But consider the following: What if individuals could, at their own speed and using their own skills, learn to feel comfortable enough to guide their financial investments using readily available news, opinions, and analysis to help them do so?

It's not only possible, but it can have the same results that software makers and online algorithm-based predictive sites do. The difference is it's done in a more methodical manner, one that keeps your gut instinct as part of the process, and does so by making it a well-informed and more confident part of the process as well.

Need an example?

What if you had recognized that the housing industry was really not taking off in 2014 as heralded, that the millennials were still avoiding home purchases, and that upscale rental properties were still going to be in great demand? What if you had researched several publicly traded companies in the real estate industry, started purchasing shares in at least one, and added to those purchases as the months went by? Suppose you were able to sell most of those shares for an average increase of over 30% the following year?

Have I got your attention?

Would it make you feel better about your ability to build your own or your family's wealth if you knew that you had followed a specific process, one grounded in long-standing methods of issue analysis that were hundreds of years old? What comfort would you take in knowing that your decisions were not based merely on numbers or algorithms but on potential investment issues that you discovered, researched, weighed, and acted upon as a result of the information that swirls around you every hour of every day?

Over recent years it has become fashionable for truly astute investors and financial pundits to suggest that relying on news reports is a risky way to create a portfolio. They indicate there is a professional way to make use of news and public opinion, and it is through sophisticated algorithms, not more rudimentary approaches, including, one would guess, common sense.

I don't buy their arguments, and this book is dedicated to showing you why. But let's not jump ahead of ourselves. Let's start with the basics, with the knowns and conventional wisdom. For a moment let's consider one by one the various reasons many argue that creating investment strategies off of news events or public opinion surveys is a bad way to go, unless it's performed by complicated computer software.

First, these experts tell you that the markets move ahead of the news. They argue that the collective wisdom of analysts and experts is far more predictive of the future price of stocks and other investment opportunities than is the news. That may be true for single events or unforeseen circumstances that spiral quickly out of control. But for one who truly dives into news and public opinion-based investing—something I call Newsvesting—it is simply incorrect that trends in the news, in politics, and in public opinion can't give an early indication of great financial opportunities or hazards that might be coming.

Second, one insider, writing in a prominent investment newsletter, *You're Not in the Loop*, explained how corporate executives, financial insiders, fund managers, and analysts know more than you. Sometimes that's true. But often they are so specialized in what they follow, or so inside their own bubbles, that they miss the overall.

Third, and the best argument for being a Newsvestor who actively engages in Newsvesting, there is too much media hype for any one person to sort through it all for relevance. That goes for general news stories as well as for those about politics and government, plus those about financial programming.

The suggestion that there is too much news out there is both true and not true. Yes, there are a lot of stories in newspapers, online, and on cable news outlets. It's tough to sort through them all. But success at Newsvesting means aggregating these stories and reports on your own, looking at the trends they suggest, and comparing them to public opinion research. That takes time, research skills, patience, and, again, common sense. These are traits that can't be replicated by a computerized algorithm.

If advanced software were capable of using information and making wise investments, one would imagine that many would have never been stuck holding certain bank stocks during and after the Great Recession of 2007–2009. And one would guess that the value placed on oil-related equities in 2014 would have seemed out of sync as well, causing these systems to dump such investments as they continued to ride high during a summer in which the price of crude was plummeting.

This is a book about how to take news, public opinion surveys, and the vast amount of information available to us and use it to create and maintain your own investment strategy.

This is not a book about algorithms or investing in commodities or playing in the futures markets. Nor is it a guide to starting businesses or investing in real estate. Those who consider themselves sophisticated Wall Street–types need to put this book down now! It might mess with your psyche too much.

Admittedly all of those facets of investing require advice from experts. In fact, even the most simple investment strategies, comprised of what most of us know something about—stocks, bonds, and relatively simple savings alternatives, such as money markets and CDs—should be done with the assistance and guidance of financial planners or those trained and licensed to trade.

Most of us are not licensed or trained in those professions, yet we still need a sound investment strategy for ourselves and our families. Quite successful people rely primarily on the advice of brokers and investment bankers in creating their portfolio, and that's great. But wouldn't it be good to know that you have a backup in determining if their advice is the right advice for you? Moreover, wouldn't it be nice to know that you could add value to those investment decisions?

Think of it like an annual physical. Everything checks out great. Heart, lungs, blood pressure, cholesterol—they're all good. One weekend you're invited to go on a ten-mile hike on a nature path with outdoorsy friends. Your doctor has told you that all your internal systems are fine. But midway through the weekend hike, your legs suggest that maybe this wasn't such a good idea. So you listen to your body and tell the others you'll have dinner ready when they return. The doctor told you that you were healthy, but your body *added value* by letting you know how far to push your good health.

In the financial world, the experts can tell us about P/E ratios and price targets for stocks, but in the end, each of us has to sign off on every investment move that is made on our behalf. To help counter all of the disclaimers investors come across while discussing the risk that comes with investing, and the lack of liability these professionals assume, we need something else to help us know that our gut instincts are backed up with more than just gut.

That's where the concept of Newsvesting comes into play. It doesn't require special software or an MBA. And if one considers just a few facts, it becomes clear that turning investing into Newsvesting makes a lot of sense and likely gives investors an edge.

This book examines Newsvesting, but to do so it requires some historical perspective. And while news is a never-ending history, the jumping-off point for this study of how news and public opinion can steer investment decisions toward enhancing wealth is the earnings reports by corporations for the first quarter of 2015.

This is a crucial point. This book is *not* just a theoretical or historical exercise. Most of the topics and investments discussed here were part of adding to portfolios that I either owned in whole or in part. And I stress that while I was responsible for the Newsvesting-based decisions to buy, sell, or hold, I always did so through experienced and qualified investment professionals.

CHAPTER **1**

The Road to Newsvesting: A Personal Journey

As a syndicated columnist, pollster, businessman, and attorney, my journey on the road to Newsvesting seemed an unlikely one. After all, I'm not an economist, nor do I have a degree in finance, and I'm certainly not a licensed investment professional. Over the years I have knocked around television newsrooms, courtrooms, and a printing plant and spent an earlier career running political campaigns. I even served in elected office.

Little did I know that all of those careers would lead to rediscovering the very essence of what one learns in those professions and applying it to a completely different world: investments.

But as a pollster, I learned one thing. Most of us who had or have investments don't really know as much as we should about what impacts our finances.

A Pew national survey taken prior to the 2012 presidential campaign found that only 14% of all American adults could answer all four of the following rather simple questions concerning the news events of the day:

+ What party controls the U.S. House of Representatives?
+ What is the general unemployment rate?
+ What nation does Angela Merkel lead?
+ Which of the two presidential nominees favors increased taxes on those who earn high incomes?

That's a sobering thought given the fact that many more than 14% of

Americans have some sort of investment, and probably many more wish they could start the process.

For those who can answer such questions, it's likely they already are Newsvestors, whether they've even heard of the term. And it would be safe to say they are among the more financially successful and stable citizens of our nation.

But with news and information coming at us so fast, even seasoned pros who devour the *Wall Street Journal* in the morning and indulge in endless hours of the Fox Business Channel, CNBC, or Bloomberg likely find it increasingly challenging to keep up with the constantly shifting sands of news and public opinion that can impact their investment strategies.

Newsvesting requires Newsvestors to not be a part of the bubble mentality that overwhelms places like Wall Street and Washington DC. In reality, people living outside of those power arenas actually have a better shot at applying news and public opinion, coupled with their own real-life experiences and gut instincts, to make smart decisions about how to build their investments.

Consider the Washington political bubble. How many times have you watched a politician advocate a policy that you knew made no sense and would never catch on? What about their ads during election time? Many of them don't address the issues you are concerned with, and most of the campaigns are focused on attacking each other so that you tire of or don't relate to anything they're saying. Have you ever asked who makes these dumb ads?

The answer is that the politicians who take positions or chase issues that never catch on and the political consultants who make these wretched campaign ads are all caught up in their own little worlds where they backslap one another and convince themselves that the public loves what they are giving them.

Sometimes not being in this elitist bubble helps. The same is true for those caught up in the bubble of an industry perspective, such as real estate developers, industry leaders, or Wall Street players.

I have been one of the relatively few writers of a nationally syndicated column about politics, business, and society in America who does not live in either Washington or New York. That's not good for growing a readership because most media want to publish columnists who frequent the DC or New York media circles and who are instantly available to appear on the various cable news shows broadcast from those areas.

That was the bad news for me as a columnist. But the good news was that I didn't have to survive in those high price markets on the relatively meager money a second-tier columnist makes. And always searching for news that was cutting edge, combined with keeping my eyes open as to how things were going in the rest of America, turned this columnist, pollster, and lawyer into an eventual avid Newsvestor.

IT'S A GRADUALLY ACQUIRED SKILL

You don't become a Newsvestor overnight. The first step is to follow the news, but not exclusively out of DC or New York. Instead, you have to look across the nation and, with our global economy, across the world.

It starts with research and keeping your own eyes open.

For me that first moment came after giving a speech in South Florida in early 2006. On the way back to the airport, I noticed numerous buildings in Miami that seemed to have uniformly spaced round lights on every floor and in every window.

I asked the person driving me why that was. He told me that those were empty high-rise condominium buildings on which construction had stopped in its tracks. To keep the skyline appearing active, the condos were required to display the lights, thousands of them, every night.

To me that was shocking, because at that very moment the housing boom across the country was reaching its apex. But seeing with my own eyes a different story caused me to research how things were going elsewhere in the allegedly red-hot housing market. It didn't take long to find news stories about a slowdown.

Within the next month I penned an article about the departure of Alan Greenspan as chairman of the Federal Reserve:

> Don't look now, but America's housing market is on the edge of a plummeting precipice. More ominous still is that it's not just the houses themselves that are a concern. All those second mortgages on homes have been serving as credit cards made not of plastic, but of brick, wood and stucco. These financial foundations may not be able to bear the weight of their debt.
>
> Recent surveys and industry reports confirm that sales of existing homes are slowing, and prices are starting to drop.

It's happening in some regions of the United States more than others, but trends are emerging.

And still, condominiums and luxury homes continue to sprout like pricey weeds. Trouble is, they are often built and bought on money borrowed to finance speculation.

The column went on to question whether this could be a nationwide implosion of the housing market and whether it could end up destroying our then-strong economy.

I didn't receive much notice for the piece, and I went back to writing weekly columns about all sorts of topics. To be honest, I didn't put my first real experience as a potential Newsvestor to any particular good use.

But by not being in the DC political or New York financial bubbles, I managed to keep my eye on the whole issue of an economic boom that had been built on the housing market. By August 2007, while the presidential candidates were bickering about immigration and Iraq, I returned to the theme I had picked up on in 2006. By now the real estate market's tumble had begun. But the news cycles continued to be dominated by more attractive issues.

In my August 16 national column for Creators Syndicate, I wrote:

Those outside the insulated bubble of Washington, DC—remember us?—nevertheless recognize the real issue for the 2008 elections.

It goes something like this: Am I about to lose everything I gained from those days when Alan Greenspan reversed the Fed's policy of instituting multiple hikes in interest rates?

You remember: The interest-rate increases Greenspan implemented to "cool off" the economy, the increases that triggered a recession.

We recovered from that Greenspan blunder only after the Great One reversed engines and started cutting interest rates as fast as he had raised them. The trouble is that this monetary finagling created a gold-rush mindset among Americans. The nation was informed that the only lasting wealth was land ownership. Land, that is, that many purchased with the bank's money, upon which borrowers then borrowed again to use as a giant credit card to pay for the good life.

Now we're seeing that the underpinnings of the American economy aren't as stout as thought. Greenspan's wild ride has left his Fed successors and government leaders with a big fat mess.

Mark it: In the coming months there's a strong likelihood that a full-blown economic panic will grip this country.

How can the economy be strong when we have lost manufacturing to other emerging nations, when we're taxing our citizens to pay for the well-being of Americans and everybody else in the world, when we have citizens with negligible personal savings, and when we have an aging population that thinks early, lavish retirement should be an entitlement?

Trust me. We're in a five-alarm financial mess. Anybody who thinks the situation is limited to the so-called "sub-prime lending" world is crazy. There are plenty of standard loans out there with borrowers worried sick about making payments— on their properties, yes, but often on home-equity loans.

And neither political party has the slightest concept of what to do. The Republicans have committed to endless war with endless costs, all the while giving huge tax breaks to oil companies.

Deal with what really matters, guys. One thousand people this week alone lost their jobs when a non-subprime lender went bankrupt.

Consumer spending and confidence are about to crash. The stock market is now artificially supported by infusions of federal cash printed so rapidly that the ink hasn't dried.

When that column was written, the Dow was trading at nearly 13,600 and the S&P closed at 1411 and change. Later in the year the S&P would rise into the 1500s, but in much of 2008 it slowly declined and oscillated between 1200 and 1400, before the near collapse of the monetary system just before the November presidential election. Obviously, the housing crisis and its ties to banks and lending in general wasn't scaring many in either the nation's top political or financial circles.

To illustrate just how much the campaigns, candidates, and reporters were missing the forest for the trees, consider that a major CNN/YouTube debate was held in Tampa, Florida, in late November 2007. Questions came from the media and from average citizens who uploaded them to YouTube. Hardly any questions centered on the housing market or subprime loans or anything related to the bombshell that would soon devastate the Tampa Bay area's housing market and seriously damage its economy for several years to come.

It was largely out of frustration with the presidential candidates who were preparing for the soon-to-be-held caucuses and primaries and their unwillingness to recognize the coming economic disaster that I made my first big move in Newsvesting and shared it with my readers in November 2007:

> Two weeks ago, I sold every stick of stock I own. That's only the second time I've done that. . . . Now we have presidential candidates still making immigration their huge issue . . . while the entire underpinnings of our economy could be washed away. . . . And what's amazing is that, based on the polls I've seen, the American people realized it long before the financial analysts or the politicians did.

This withdrawal from the market was a decision I never regretted, and within a year it was one that made me a Newsvestor for life. But I first had to learn a tough lesson about not being a disciplined Newsvestor.

NOT SO SMART AFTER ALL— A SHOVE INTO NEWSVESTING

On February 7, 2008, newspapers and news networks were absorbed in the battle for the Republican and Democratic presidential nominations. The issues were the same ones the candidates had been speaking about for well over a year.

But something started happening on that day that sealed the deal for me and my decision to be a more dedicated Newsvestor. Early in that month an entire investment vehicle that had been portrayed by most investment banks as the equivalent of a money market, known as auction rate securities (ARS), began to encounter trouble. According to some, the ARS had been invented in the 1980s by an expert at the leading Wall Street firm known as Lehman Brothers.

Basically, auction rate securities took long-term debt instruments—for example, municipal bonds—and regularly reset that particular instrument's interest rate at private auctions. The auctions were typically held every seven, twenty-eight, or thirty-five days, with interest being paid at the end of the short period that the bond or other form of paper was held.

Investment firms marketed these securities as an alternative to typical money markets, yielding higher rates of return and declaring them to be just as safe. But there was one problem. In February 2008, the auctions were held as usual, but *no one* was willing to bid. Within a short time, 80% of those auctions failed to have any participants.

As the ARS market seized up, many high-wealth investors who had parked money in these accounts saw the ARS's value marked down to virtually nothing. And by the time the story of the failure of the ARS market reached widespread coverage, the entire U.S. monetary system was under the gun and dominated the front pages.

And that brilliant move I made in 2007 while the markets were riding high—the one to sell all of my stock—well, it didn't seem so brilliant when I realized that my money was allegedly safely parked in those so-called investment bank money markets made up entirely of auction rate securities. By the end of 2008, the nation's economy had suffered a complete meltdown, and the S&P closed for the year at 890.

As the crisis played itself out, I held my breath. My particular investment bank had continued to show the ARS account at nearly full value, stating that they would make good on their value. But other big Wall Street names were sending their clients with ARS accounts monthly statements showing zero value. I entered the words *auction rate securities* into my search engine news alerts . . . and held my breath.

I didn't breath easily again until then–New York State attorney general Andrew Cuomo threatened the investment houses with draconian punishment if they did not stand by their creative versions of the money market. As a conservative columnist with a Republican history, I owe a debt of thanks to AG Cuomo, who comes from a distinguished Democrat and probably more left-of-center political family. That made little difference to me. He had preserved my funds and later was elected governor of his state.

As I ventured closer to becoming a dedicated Newsvestor, I learned another valuable lesson in Newsvesting: keep up with the news on every aspect of your investment portfolio, even parts that seem safe, like money markets, or others that pretend to be safe and solid.

As we slowly emerged from the heavy days of the Great Recession, one thing was clear: not paying attention to the news—whether it be political, financial, or social—has devastating consequences. And climbing out of the rubble, particularly as the markets appeared to be recovering much faster than the millions of Americans who had been left behind during the Great Recession, convinced me it was time to put some order in place, a method to the madness, of digesting information and building investments for the future.

I decided to merge my training as a high school debater (which had led to my years in politics first as a debate assistant to newly elected Republican Congressman Newt Gingrich) and as a law student and lawyer with the valuable methodology and value for public opinion I gained in my years as a pollster.

But first I had to reconcile the many rules that seemed to govern prudent investing. There was another step to take before Newsvesting could truly spring to life for me.

CHAPTER **2**

Newsvesting in Action

Before someone decides to become a Newsvestor, or even takes the time to learn the process, it would help to see a Newsvesting opportunity and how it can add value to a portfolio of stock.

As I will explain later, I do not advocate day trading or even short-term swing trading. But if news events start to unfold in a manner that can lower the market in general, or a particular segment or sector, that can be a Newsvesting event.

A textbook case of how headlines can affect the stock market arose over a nine-day span in October 2014. That's when a mixture of panic and paranoia gripped the United States—and many investors. It was a double whammy of "new news"—geopolitical events that until that time were largely unknown to most Americans. The result was a drop in the Dow Jones of 877 points over a nine-day period, from 16,994 on October 8 to 16,117 on October 16.

The first big story was a spate of military conquests by the barbaric militant Islamist group ISIS, or the Islamic State. ISIS had been known to Western authorities at least since the previous year, but those Americans who had paid any attention at all had been reassured by President Obama's dismissal of ISIS on January 14 as Islamic terror's "junior varsity team."

All the more terrifying was an unexpected wave of new conquests by ISIS, especially in Iraq, the site of America's long and bloody but ultimately victorious war of previous years. By October 2014, however, it appeared that areas apparently pacified by the U.S. military were suddenly under the control of an army that glorified in enslaving women and children and in beheading prisoners and webcasting the executions on the Internet.

It's no stretch to say that these terrorists were indeed spreading terror, or at least anxiety, among Americans. By mid-October there was a vague feeling in the United States and in the West that ISIS was a plague of barbarism starting to rage out of control. Consider this succession of headlines and news stories over a twelve-day stretch:

+ Huffington Post, October 3: "Corporal Jordan Spears Is First U.S. Death In Operations Against ISIS"
+ Fox News, October 8: "Congressman: 'At least 10 ISIS fighters caught trying to cross into US'"
+ NBC Nightly News, October 8: "ISIS Imitators Discussed Attacks on U.S. Targets in Canada"
+ CNN, October 14: "10/14 Battle for Syria's Kobani intensifies; ISIS takes Iraq base"
+ CNN, October 14: "Obama on ISIS: Expect 'long-term campaign'"

But for investors, ISIS wasn't the only bad news coming down the pike that month. While there were claims that ISIS fighters might be stealing across the border into the United States, there was another potentially more lethal "enemy" that had already arrived stateside: Ebola.

A *Wikipedia* article explained in a nutshell how the spread of Ebola in West Africa in 2014 reached the United States in late 2014: "On September 30, 2014, the CDC announced (a male) 42-year-old (later corrected by CDC reports as 45 years old) Liberian national visiting the United States from Liberia, had been diagnosed with Ebola in Dallas, Texas. He had been visiting family in Dallas, was treated at Texas Health Presbyterian Hospital Dallas. By October 4, (his) condition had deteriorated from 'serious but stable' to 'critical.' On October 8, (the man) died of Ebola." Three other Ebola cases were diagnosed in the United States that month.

Americans were alarmed over the seemingly fatal and fast-moving virus reaching the United States, and it became obvious that airlines were going to take a serious hit based on the global nature of air travel.

BusinessInsider.com reported on Monday, October 13: "It's been a terrible couple of days for the airlines, with each of these stocks losing more than 13% over the past five trading days, with American Airlines' 19% decline over that period outpacing peers."

A report from Bloomberg that same Monday said that officials at the CDC rejected calls from some lawmakers to impose travel bans as the Ebola outbreak spread from West Africa to the United States and Europe.

BusinessInsider.com also reported on that Monday the identity of a second Ebola patient in Dallas: "Nina Pham, 26, is reportedly a nurse in Dallas who was caring for Ebola patient Thomas Eric Duncan at Texas Health Presbyterian Hospital.

"Monday's decline in airline stocks came after last week a number of travel companies focused on Europe, including International Consolidated Airlines, which owns British Airways, and Carnival Cruises, saw shares fall after the first case of Ebola was confirmed in Spain."

The news for airlines didn't get any better.

The *Washington Post* and other news organizations around the world reported on Wednesday morning, October 15, "The second healthcare worker diagnosed with Ebola had a fever of 99.5 degrees Fahrenheit before boarding a passenger jet on Monday, a day before she reported symptoms of the virus and was tested, according to public health officials."

By midday, follow-up stories were running on online sites and on cable news shows, and the story was going truly viral.

A good example is a story posted that afternoon on Newsmax: "Concerns over the spread of Ebola have stretched from Texas to Ohio after it was learned that the second healthcare worker to contract the deadly disease flew from Cleveland to Dallas one day before she was diagnosed." The Newsmax story quoted the head of the CDC as saying it was highly unlikely that other passengers could have been infected during the flight. But that was hardly comforting to those who were on the flight or for that matter to anyone who might be traveling.

The story continued: "The Ohio Health Department said it is tracing the contacts of Texas nurse Amber Vinson and is working with Frontier Airlines officials to track down additional people the nurse may have come into contact with." On Newsmax, Wisconsin Senator Ron Johnson said, "The CDC and the Obama administration need to be upfront about how exactly the two healthcare workers contracted the virus."

CDC director Thomas Frieden, in a news conference that day, said, "She was in a group of individuals known to have exposure to Ebola. . . . Even though there appeared to be little risk for the other people on that flight, she should not have traveled that way. . . . CDC guidelines outline the need for 'controlled movement,' and that does not include taking any kind of public transportation."

American Airlines was, prior to the Ebola crisis, considered a leader in an industry that has seen its ups and downs. Most analysts had either a strong buy or a buy rating on the stock. While there are numerous places to examine analyst views on a certain company and how they expect shares of stock to trade in the near or longer term, YahooFinance.com, FoxBusiness.com, and CNBC.com are just three examples.

Generally I'm not a fan of airline stocks because they are one or two accidents from major problems. But the Ebola crisis presented a unique opportunity to invest during a major (and sadly tragic) news story that logic suggested would ultimately turn out in a manner that certainly would not hurt airlines any more than the market as a whole.

Working with my investment advisor (it is never a good idea not to have professional assistance), who happened to be in my office as the news hit of the Ebola patient who had flown with a fever but before developing other symptoms, we seized the moment. American Airlines, which had been trading at a comfortable cruising altitude of around $40 a share in early September 2014, plunged during the Ebola scare, along with the price of shares of other major airlines.

I bought 625 shares of AAL at $31.66 on the afternoon of October 15. I sold it all six days later at a price of $37.66 per share. So in six trading days, as the panic began to subside, American Airlines was climbing back up and I had banked a $6-a-share profit.

This was almost emergency type Newsvesting, and not the norm, but it proved the system to be pretty sound. (Stay tuned for the full Newsvesting process.)

Even though, as mentioned earlier, I'm not a day trader, and Newsvesting is meant to be for long-term investments, my general concern about owning airline stocks (a personal issue) made this an investment based on news stories and some logical analysis a pretty easy one to make. And it proved the system to be reliable.

While it was unclear as to when the government would take firm action to keep those exposed to Ebola off of planes, it made sense that if these cases started appearing in high numbers, drastic measures would have to be taken. Yes, there could be further declines in AAL's stock price. But I was prepared to dollar average my cost of AAL by purchasing more shares at certain lower thresholds. After all, if people started contracting Ebola in the United States in numerous locations and at a more rapid rate, the airlines would likely not suffer more than other sectors of the economy. In fact, because of the nature of air travel and security measures, airlines would be more capable of controlling the situation than larger venues, such as ballparks and shopping malls.

Even if it had taken months to get an Ebola epidemic under control, stock prices in general would become much less expensive over all, and once we emerged from any prolonged crisis, it would be likely that the otherwise strengthening economy would take hold again, and stock prices in general would rise.

That took care of the airlines. ISIS, however, was a different matter.

The growing threat of ISIS (or ISIL, as President Obama called it) was equally as troubling and at the same time presented a Newsvestment opportunity. ISIS was on the move and declared itself the Islamic State in the summer of 2014. It kidnapped individuals from developed nations and demanded huge ransoms. Its military forces advanced and overwhelmed certain territorial areas of Iraq. By October 2014, its troops had advanced to within twenty-five miles of Baghdad. But while ISIS had been on my Newsvesting radar for over a year, it seemed not to gain prominence with the more general news sources until the summer of 2014, and even then only sporadically.

We know that all news is cyclical. After dominating headlines for years after the tragedy of 9/11, Al-Qaeda slowly drifted off the front pages, replaced by references to the Taliban and later ISIS. In 2014, with both Ebola and ISIS dominating the news, a stock market that had ignored international issues for the most part in recent years was predictably headed toward a temporary decline.

To capture what I anticipated to be a broad decline in stocks, I turned to a vehicle I usually avoid—exchange traded funds (ETFs). The popular investment site MotleyFool.com explains ETFs best: "What exactly is an exchange-traded fund (ETF)? 'Exchange-traded' refers to shares that trade all day long on the major stock market exchanges (just like regular stocks). 'Funds' are investing vehicles that hold dozens, hundreds, or even thousands of companies under one umbrella unified by a particular investing theme (such as companies that comprise the Dow)."

There are ETFs for all sectors of the market, and they have been wildly popular since their emergence in the 1990s. I shy away from them because I believe in investing in a business, not a pack of businesses that happen to do the same thing. That being said, many investment experts argue that ETFs outperform handpicked portfolios.

But in the instance of what seemed an extraordinarily news-driven decline in the market, I felt I could capture that decline (buy when others are selling, as famed investor Warren Buffett teaches) through an ETF that comprises a broad segment of the S&P 500 (SPY). We purchased two tranches of SPY in October—one prior to the October 15 disclosure of the feverish Ebola patient on an airplane, and one that day. I used the second purchase to dollar-cost average my total investment in SPY.

What is dollar-cost averaging? *Wikipedia* defines it well: "Dollar cost averaging (DCA) is an investment strategy for reducing the impact of volatility on large purchases of financial assets such as equities. By dividing the total sum to be invested in the market (e.g. $100,000) into equal amounts put into the market at regular intervals (e.g. $1000 over 100 weeks), DCA reduces the risk of incurring a substantial loss resulting from investing the entire 'lump sum' just before a fall in the market. Dollar cost averaging is not always the most profitable way to invest a large sum, but it minimizes downside risk."

For me the most important part of that description is "minimizes downside risk." My view is that I never want to be overly ambitious in trying to score a huge victory with an investment. My motto is: "I'm happy with the child's portion." If you get enough of that smaller portion of profits, you will find that you have more and more cash with which to invest in other opportunities, and your smaller but less risky portions will become larger over time.

I struck quickly. Within a matter of days my dollar-cost average in SPY was a little over $191 a share. I held the stock until both ISIS and Ebola had moved off the front pages, and on January 29, 2015, I sold my shares for $206 a share. Basically, in three months' time and with a willingness to keep purchasing had the market tanked, I was able to see a profit of around $15 per share.

I could have held on and potentially ridden those shares up to a much higher level. But by Memorial Day, the unofficial start of summer, shares of

SPY were only $6 higher. I pocketed my Newsvesting profits and moved on to put that cash to work elsewhere. Yes, my profits would be taxed at ordinary income rates under the current treatment of short-term capital gains. But for around three months of not-so-hard work, I was happy to take my profits and avoid potential future risks.

After all, I had much more Newsvesting to do.

ISSUE 1 ISIS Emerges

INITIAL EVIDENCE

Oct 1, 2013, *NYTimes*: "Since the group . . . ISIS announced its presence in Syria this year . . . it has emerged as a leading force exploiting chaos into jihad."

Washington Post: "Increased concern about ISIS..."

EXTENDED EVIDENCE

July 17, 2014, Reuters: "Saudi Arabia boosts security in Iraq frontier (as ISIS takes key Iraqi areas)."

October 11, 2014, numerous news sources: "ISIS attempts to take Baghdad."

ISSUE 2 Ebola

INITIAL EVIDENCE

July 29, 2014, NBC Nightly News: "(Ebola) Devastating where it is located, becoming out of control (in some locations in Africa). First American has died there."

August 2, 2014, *Wall Street Journal*: "Two U.S. patients will be flown to Atlanta to be treated."

EXTENDED EVIDENCE

October 13, 2014, *Washington Times*: "1st US patient with Ebola enters Texas hospital."

October 14, 2014, numerous news sources: "Nurse who cares for Texas patient contracts Ebola."

October 15, 2014, *Washington Post*: "2nd healthcare worker contracts Ebola . . . flew on airline with fever two days earlier."

October 15, 2015, Newsmax: "Concern over Ebola stretches from Texas to Ohio where flight of Ebola patient originated."

ISSUE 1 ISIS Emerges

ANALYSIS	CONCLUSION/ACTION	RESULT
ISIS now dominates news. Financial papers, sites, and programs now focus on.	On October 16, 2014, purchased SPY (SPDR Trust Index Series 1) at $191.80.	Sell SPY on December 19, 2014, at $208.78, with an 8.85% return in two months.

ISSUE 2 Ebola

ANALYSIS	CONCLUSION/ACTION	RESULT
Ebola crisis concerns reach height. Panic over airlines and Ebola will hit airline stocks, but ultimately airline/airport security can control better than larger public locations if Ebola becomes huge crisis.	Purchase American Airlines (AAL) as price drops on news of Ebola patient having flown emerges during the day. Purchase shares in American Airlines at $31.66.	Sell American Airlines October 21, 2014, at $37.78.

CHAPTER **3**

Using *Your* Head (or Somebody Else's)

Conventional wisdom (CW), that oft-quoted, wise, anonymous sage of counsel and advice, holds that the best way to increase your wealth through investments is to buy low and sell high. Well, duh. That's kind of like saying, "Don't lean into a left hook," or following pitcher Satchel Paige's rule, "Don't look back! Something might be gaining on you." In either case, it's easier said than done.

Investment advisor Tristan Yates added to the obvious CW in an article in Investopedia entitled "4 Ways to Predict Market Performance." (We'll get to those in a moment.) Yates said, "There are two prices that are critical for any investor to know: the current price of the investment he or she owns, or plans to own, and its future selling price." That kind of knowledge would certainly simplify investing, wouldn't it?

Yates, of course, had a lot more to say on the subject, as his article looked at "four different views of the market [to] learn more about the associated academic research that supports each view." The goal was to "help you better understand how the market functions, and perhaps eliminate some of your own biases."

Momentum, mean reversion, martingales, and the search for value headline Yates's differing views of the market.

Here's his take on momentum:

"Don't fight the tape." This widely quoted piece of stock market wisdom warns investors not to get in the way of market trends. The assumption is that the best bet about market movements is that they will continue to go in the same direction. This concept has its roots in behavioral finance. With so many stocks to choose from, why would investors keep their money in a stock that's falling, as opposed to one that's climbing? It's classic fear and greed.

(Note: Investopedia defines "behavioral finance" as "A field of finance that proposes psychology-based theories to explain stock market anomalies. Within behavioral finance, it is assumed that the information structure and the characteristics of market participants systematically influence individuals' investment decisions as well as market outcomes.")

In this scenario, the suggestion is a "positive feedback loop" wherein as people see positive returns, they continue to invest, the market goes up, and more investment takes place. But as Yates found in an older study, while that might be good for the short term, "stocks that have performed well in the past three to five years are more likely to underperform the market in the next three to five years and vice versa."

That led him to mean reversion:

Experienced investors who have seen many market ups and downs, often take the view that the market will even out, over time. Historically high market prices often discourage these investors from investing, while historically low prices may represent an opportunity.

The tendency of a variable, such as a stock price, to converge on an average value over time is called mean reversion. The phenomenon has been found in several economic indicators, including exchange rates, gross domestic product (GDP) growth, interest rates and unemployment. Mean reversion may also be responsible for business cycles.

Even after decades of research, Yates stated that numbers are "still inconclusive about whether stock prices revert to the mean." His hardly definitive conclusion on the subject was that "if the market does have a tendency to mean revert, it is a phenomenon that happens slowly and almost imperceptibly, over many years or even decades."

Ready for more? Like I said, I'm not an economist, but it's important to know where you've come from to help decide where you're going, especially when it comes to your investments.

According to Yates, "Another possibility (regarding stock predicting) is that past returns just don't matter." He cited a 1965 Paul Samuelson study on market returns that "found that past pricing trends had no effect on future prices," and he reasoned that "in an efficient market, there should be no such effect." His conclusion was that market prices are martingales.

So what's a martingale? Yates said it's "a mathematical series in which the best prediction for the next number is the current number." He further explained (thank goodness), "The concept is used in probability theory, to estimate the results of random motion. For example, suppose that you have $50 and bet it all on a coin toss. How much money will you have after the toss? You could have $100 or you may have $0 after the toss, but statistically the best prediction is $50; your original starting position. The prediction of your fortunes after the toss is a martingale."

If stock returns are martingales, then this theory holds that a current price and possible volatility are all you need to know. Past trends don't matter. Again, according to Yates, "If stock returns are essentially random, the best predictions for tomorrow's market price is simply today's price, plus a very small increase. Rather than focusing on past trends and looking for possible momentum or mean reversion, investors should instead concentrate on managing the risk inherent in their volatile investments."

Finally, there's the search for value. This one's pretty obvious and goes along with the "buy low, sell high" CW mantra. "Value investors," Yates said,

> Purchase stock cheaply and expect to be rewarded later. Their hope is that an inefficient market has underpriced the stock, but that the price will adjust over time. The question is does this happen and why would an inefficient market make this adjustment?
>
> Research suggests that this mispricing and readjustment consistently happens, although it presents very little evidence for why it happens. . . . The only conclusion that could be

drawn is that these stocks have extra risk, for which investors demand additional compensation.

In economic-speak, Yates suggested, "Price is the driver of the valuation ratios, therefore, the findings do support the idea of a mean-reverting stock market. As prices climb, the valuation ratios get higher and, as a result, future predicted returns are lower. However, the market P/E ratio has fluctuated widely over time and has never been a consistent buy or sell signal."

Did you get all that? Obviously, there are myriad ways to go about investing. But after looking at these basics, what does that leave you with? Yates summed it up this way: "There are no solid answers." Well, surprise, surprise.

And it all leaves the door wide open to using your own head and your own gut to make intelligent and, hopefully, profitable Newsvestments.

RECONCILING NEWSVESTING WITH PROFESSIONAL INVESTING

The man who came to symbolize prudent and astute investors, Warren Buffett, became the ultimate rock star among those who follow the world of investments, with his set of investment guidelines or rules that he stuck to for years. Basically his philosophy was that of investing in quality businesses and holding on to these stocks for a very long time. He hasn't been big on jumping in and out of the market, and he generally has avoided stock-market forecasts and the talking heads, likely because of the echo chamber they create.

Buffett's Berkshire Hathaway Inc. is a multinational conglomerate holding company that oversees and manages a number of subsidiary companies. According to *Wikipedia*, in 2015, "the company wholly owns GEICO, BNSF, Lubrizol, Dairy Queen, Fruit of the Loom, Helzberg Diamonds, FlightSafety International, and NetJets, owns half of Heinz and an undisclosed percentage of Mars, Incorporated, and has significant minority holdings in American Express, The Coca-Cola Company, Wells Fargo, IBM and Restaurant Brands International. Berkshire Hathaway averaged an annual growth in book value of 19.7% to its shareholders for the last 49 years (compared to 9.8% from the S&P 500 with dividends included for the same period), while employing large amounts of capital, and minimal debt."

Pretty darned impressive.

But while Warren Buffett is a self-made man, he managed to create some capital to work with at an extremely young age. That gave him a means to put his theories to work in a practical and real sense. For some it is hard enough to figure out how to find capital they can invest in the first place, much less to know where to put it if they save enough to become an investor. For others, larger investors with strong resources, the battle becomes one of how to see their investments grow, and later in life how to preserve the body of their wealth while deriving enough income from it to live whatever lifestyle they anticipate having in the years to come. For large institutional investors the issues are far more complex.

Warren Buffett appeared to develop some rules as an investor that might seem contradictory to others. For example, while he was known for ignoring the experts who bought equities based on charts, or so-called technicals, he advocated that investors read and watch everything possible to form their own opinions as to what to invest in and when. And most important, Buffett's approach was to view major downturns in the market, in certain sectors, or even individual stocks, as buying opportunities. In essence, he took advantage of good opportunities to buy while others were panicking and selling.

In his book *How Buffett Does It*, James Pardoe boiled the basic strategies of the man who would become America's most legendary investor into twenty-four basic rules of the financial road.

At first, one might think many of the strategies Buffett employed, as described by Pardoe, to be counter to the concept of Newsvesting. But in reality, most of Buffett's long-held beliefs bolster the argument that we should all be Newsvestors.

To avoid the echo chambers, or as I describe them, the bubbles of the DC and Wall Street crowds, Buffett believed that after reading and watching everything an investor could, they should ultimately make their own decisions about where to put their money. For the Newsvestor that's extremely important, because by engaging in true Newsvesting, you bring more to the table than most. The best mix for a Newsvestor, is the advice of a well-trained professional who will not try to override you but who can add traditional market analysis to help Newsvesting work. In the end, anyone using news and public opinion data must balance that with details about how a company or other investment is run, its debt, its cash flow, its P/E ratio, its dividends, and much more to make a final gut decision.

Perhaps Buffett's most enduring principle is that an investor is never just buying equity or stock; you are actually buying part of a company. That means feeling good about the actual entity, who runs it, and how it is run. For Newsvestors, that means going the extra mile. A Newsvestor might like a certain stock, but when researching the company, she may find that it generally gets bad reviews from consumers who buy its products. While the analysts on Wall Street might sing the company's praises, the Newsvestor might skip purchasing shares in such a company.

Another rule that Buffett operated by was not to jump in and out of the market. In this instance, Newsvesting both augments this concept and slightly challenges it. The goal of using news and public opinion trends to guide either creating your own portfolio or to build upon it is to seek out strong long-term investments in strong companies and, as often as possible, ones that pay out a reasonable dividend/yield. That means sticking with these choices and being paid something, usually on a quarterly basis, for putting your faith and money into them.

But Newsvesting is important to a newcomer to the world of investing as well as those who have built their nest eggs because it can, in very real ways, help a newcomer choose a time to dive into what might be a red-hot market at a time when the cost of certain good stocks might temporarily dip on bad news or when there is a temporary shift in consumer or public opinion.

While the idea of never touching one's investments, even as the world seems to be melting along with the value of your investments, sounds reasonable, given that the market historically rebounds and goes to greater heights, it's not always practical. And that approach can sometimes rob true Newsvestors of opportunities to take advantage of their diligence.

The truth in the use of news and opinion in choosing times to get into or out of the market or a given investment is the truth about virtually everything in life: moderation.

Consider the Bank of America. Look at the date when I wrote that column about selling all of my shares in every stock I owned: August 2007. Bank of America was flying high, like most big banks. Throughout August it bounced around at prices in the upper $40 range and by September had crossed $50 a share.

But by the time the economic meltdown of 2008 hit and the dust had settled, Bank of America closed on December 1, 2008, at just above $14! By the spring of 2015 the stock was stuck in the $16 range.

That's not to say that down the road we won't see Bank of America spring back to life. But the value in being a Newsvestor, willing to pull a trigger long ahead of a crowd, is fairly obvious. And it fits with the Buffett rules set forth in Pardoe's book, in which the author noted that Buffett followed a pattern of buying when other people were selling and selling when others were buying.

Since most folks don't have the resources of Warren Buffett, they instead require the use of tools like Newsvesting to sense an opportunity to get out of a particular investment while the getting is good in order to have resources to buy when others are selling. Doing so requires sorting through a lot of opinion. That's where the Newsvestor approach comes into play. *It's an approach that requires applying news, facts, and opinions while remaining grounded in the real world.* And that's an approach that is rarer than one might guess.

AVOIDING THE BUBBLE

Everyone has an opinion as to what policies should be implemented and what political candidates should say or do what. And many times the results are completely different from what the experts predict. But just as is the case in the political world, there are some trends and even results that a trained eye can pretty much forecast far ahead of the final outcome. Most of the more predictable moments in politics result from various cycles in national news and from shifts in public opinion.

But for some who are caught up in the political world, either as candidates, consultants, elected officials, or political pundits on television or in newspapers, what should seem obvious often gets lost in the echo chamber of the political world. So many political careers end because of a failure to avoid focusing on the inside. Too many politicians miss the obvious political freight train created by an issue, by a shift in public opinion, by pushing bad legislation, or even by running bad commercials during campaign season.

As to financial news programming, newspapers, and online content, just as everyone seems to have an expert opinion as to politics, most everyone who follows the world of finance and investing has an opinion as to how the markets will perform and where both large institutional investors and average investors should put their money to enjoy both growth and perhaps a good return in the form of a dividend or coupon as well.

It's interesting to realize that, just as is the case with politics, average investors can often be more successful in making decisions about investments than the experts on Wall Street by following the news or even by listening to their friends, acquaintances, and colleagues.

Even investment newsletters take a stab at trying to guess the future. One at the end of 2014 reported these major predictions for 2015:

+ America's debt reckoning will force gold to soar to $11,250.
+ A national currency is doomed to fail and how to profit from its demise.
+ The Islamic State will push oil to unseen levels, decimating U.S. GDP.
+ A trend that predicts the end of the dollar's rally.

It doesn't appear that many of those predictions were proving accurate by mid-2015.

It's pretty clear there are no magic potions when it comes to accumulating wealth or taking what someone has and preserving or growing it. And there is no shortage of self-help books or television ads that purport to be the answer to financial success and security. Some are better than others. But many a person has hopped on the gold train during times when the price of gold was rising only to find out that they hopped on too late. That doesn't mean get-rich ads for investing in gold are necessarily always bad. But it illustrates the point that often, if an investment is on fire and you are just learning about it, you probably have missed the opportunity to enjoy its real upside.

All one needs to do is watch the various financial cable programs to realize that news and public opinion impact corporations and investments more than any other single factor. Add the government's influence, both with laws and policies, and you have the crux of what really moves the direction that companies, stocks, bonds, commodities—you name it—ultimately take.

These various television networks and online entities provide an invaluable service to America's financial institutions. They have brought a huge, bright, and ever-changing spotlight to what used to be exclusively the domain of old-fashioned stock tickers, corporate and annual reports, and relatively small business sections in print newspapers. For many decades, only financial newspapers such as the *Wall Street Journal* and monthly magazines such a *Forbes, Fortune,* and *Businessweek* provided up-to-date information about the worlds of business and finance. Now, online and broadcast media provide moment-by-moment news and analysis of virtually every industry and segment of our financial markets.

But for those who seek to rely solely on the daily programs devoted to business and finance, there is one thing to keep in mind. Most producers of the various shows that air on these networks like to provide two sides to most issues and ideas. If they don't do so in one particular segment of a program, they will balance out opinions on a later broadcast. To true devotees of these shows and their networks, that can become a confusing echo chamber. While these programs are valuable, as are the many online sites devoted to business and finance, there has to be some way to sift through all the information and opinions in order to get a clearer picture of what and when to buy, sell, or hold.

So when the experts warn against using the news, be it political or financial, in determining investments, they seemingly have a valid point. But they are missing the fact that people who are not in the DC or Wall Street bubbles have a better chance of using their everyday experiences, along with a few simple tools available to everyone, to create an opportunity to let the news work for them. To start Newsvesting and doing so successfully.

CHAPTER **4**

How to Start Newsvesting

READ, READ, READ

Right up front, here's the best part: you don't need sophisticated software and algorithms to engage in a simple but dedicated system of Newsvesting. In fact, it could easily be argued that the decision to become a Newsvestor may be even more important as automated computer systems used to buy and sell equities become more commonplace.

Consider a front-page *Wall Street Journal* story in early 2015 that focused on a firm where dozens of PhDs huddle around computers to search the newswires and earnings reports, plus everything from weather reports to Twitter, to use in algorithms designed to make stock picks from the signals the data provides.

There is little doubt that these highly advanced computer systems will be a wave of the future. The proponents of such systems argue that the markets can be predicted, if not 100% of the time, then enough to make substantial profits. And they vary as to how they operate. For example, one company provides analysis based on news and data, which leads to automated buying and selling based on the weighting of the multiple levels and types of data produced. Another system operates on broader categories, leaving less to the computers in making final conclusions or determining a set system of analysis.

While this quantitative investing, and in particular quantitative programs that rely on news-related information in real time, is likely to become standard fare in the years to come, it is not, by and large, easily available to individual investors. And the one issue that remains a sticking point for many who skeptically view these systems is that of the actual strength of correlation between any given set of news, financial information, and other data versus the strength of that correlation as provided by mathematical formulas. (Could it be that the computer nerds really *don't* know everything?)

While those boosting media and news-based algorithms question why anyone would ever invest on gut instinct rather than a set formula, the reality is that in almost every aspect of life, there is a point at which human judgment, based on logic or instinct or a combination of both, plays a role. The most logic-based competition in the world, namely, competitive academic debate, relies on identifiable issues, facts, propositions, and arguments as well as facts in opposition to the propositions, and ultimately, a decision by a human serving as a judge, to determine the winner of the contest. Along the way, the contestants must establish the strength of the causality between the facts or evidence they rely on and the result or effect they argue to be likely when considering those facts.

That's much like how a jury weighs testimony and evidence, governed by a set of rules as to what evidence may be considered. Most decisions, even those involving life and death, require people, not computers, to weigh the evidence and make a choice.

As a Newsvestor and an individual, it is impossible to gather the massive amount of real-time data that these complicated computerized systems amass. And there are no debaters, lawyers, or advocates present to make the case for or against an investment move. But by filtering information down to a manageable level, determining issues that might relate to areas of investment or levels to which one invests, one can apply a fairly simple but logical ongoing debate where news, opinion, financial information, and other reliable and consistent sources can be applied and decisions can be made with a stronger likelihood of positive financial results—both long-term and occasionally on a short-term basis.

The good news is that you are your own boss in deciding what sources of news, public opinion, and statistics to use in the process. In the end, your investment decisions are determined by taking the process of Newsvesting, using good advice from your financial consultant, broker, or investment advisor, and then going with your gut, based on the balancing test that Newsvestors use.

AN OVERVIEW TO THE NEWSVESTING PROCESS

Newsvesting is rooted in several different forms of critical analysis, all of which assist in making a decision as to when and where to invest, and to assist in deciding, on rare occasions, when to take money out of various investments and where best to park it.

In Newsvesting it's best to consider news, opinion, and data as a matter of balance. Virtually every form of competitive critical thinking requires balancing evidence and data and determining what side outweighs the other. That's the case in aforementioned competitive debates, legal trials, and even presidential debates and campaigns. In the end someone has to gather facts, determine what the issues are, analyze them, and reach a definitive conclusion.

Many who have attended law school were taught the IRAC method of analyzing complex legal matters. IRAC stands for issue, rule, application, and conclusion.

While some law schools and professors have abandoned IRAC, most successful lawyers and professionals use a form of this time-honored system. Those who criticize the method believe it leads to an oversimplification of proper legal analysis. That may be the case in the world of law-school academia, but in the world where real problems present themselves rapidly, the IRAC method is very reliable.

In many ways IRAC is incredibly similar to the rules of academic competitive debate. And that's what Newsvesting boils down to. Making an informed decision based on a set of rules for identifying an investment issue or opportunity, gathering evidence related to the issue, charting the pros and cons, weighing the evidence, and then making an investment decision. For me, Newsvesting is the equivalent of a highly competitive policy debate—the type one might see occur between debaters that compete at a high level of competence—combined with the IRAC legal method.

If those approaches sound too theoretical and impractical in determining what news and other information might be useful in helping to form an investment strategy, consider how the news you view on television every evening is created.

Planning for a news broadcast, be it national or local, requires shifts of producers, editors, and reporters who fill conference rooms or share teleconferences in which the old-fashioned assignment board or its electronic version is filled out. The same type of information Newsvestors will use is gathered at various times of the day, and decisions are made as to what stories (issues) will make a given broadcast. The story is assigned, and reporters and other staff work to put the story together. The unspoken rule that is applied in this case is the combination of interviews and text that are interwoven into the particular news story. In the academic debate world, that would be considered the evidence.

Under the IRAC method, the next step would be the *application* of the existing law. In news reports that would likely be additional facts, including an explanation of how a news story may move forward. For example, "It's up to the Supreme Court to now rule on this pressing issue."

And whether they mean to or not, most news stories reach a *conclusion*, even if in many cases it appears that no opinion is offered. Watch any news story and you will likely come away with an idea of how that story might end up. It's subtle, and not so subtle in some instances, but it's usually there.

To create a Newsvesting formula, I merged the rules of academic debate, the IRAC method, and a general manner in which news organizations sort through a sea of stories to create the issues of the day in order to establish a consistent process that any investor can use, regardless of his experience with debates or lawyers or newsrooms. And the best news is that it doesn't require algorithms or mathematical equations. All that is required is consistent research, a willingness to understand a bit of modern history and to follow the Newsvesting system, plus some common sense.

STEP 1 GETTING THE BASICS DOWN—A MACRO VIEW

This is undoubtedly the most difficult part of using the Newsvesting approach and making investment decisions. If you already own stocks or other investment vehicles, such as municipal or corporate bonds, as part of your portfolio or as an area of interest, that makes Newsvesting a bit easier.

All too often people enter the investment world with no concept of what to invest in or when to enter a particular market. That's why I strongly urge anyone interested in creating wealth through investments to seek professional assistance. You might ask, why worry about being a Newsvestor if you are going to have to rely on a financial advisor, planner, or broker? The point is that the expert provides you with a good sense of the general view of various markets. Their advice as to what or when to buy might be hit or miss, but getting a feel for the investment landscape from experts is a great way to launch your own investment strategy.

Consider these professionals as coaches, mentors, advisors, or professors. Just do not let them make any final decisions for you.

If you're already invested in stocks, bonds, or some alternative investments, then the Newsvesting concept takes on the additional role of keeping track of those investments, determining when to augment or diversify them, and in rare instances when to escape to safer financial territory.

The first step is to get a macro view of the markets, the economy (both domestic and foreign), and a sense of the political environment (in the United States and in various parts of the world). That's a lot of work, but here's how to get started.

First, be sure you know what the current interest rates are and in which direction they are moving. Know the strength of the dollar versus other currencies, the unemployment rate, and a year's worth of gross domestic product quarterly reports (revised and most recent quarter). While that sounds like simple stuff, remember that fewer than 14% of Americans could correctly answer something as simple as the general unemployment rate when asked in a national survey.

Obviously full-time investors can recite the performance of various markets chapter and verse over many years. But for those who are not full-time pros, it's important to get a feel for how the various markets have performed in the past.

Start with the longest view, that being a chart of the performance of the Dow, NASDQ, and S&P going back at least ten years. If you have any sense of general history, you will quickly note the times when the markets, or at least one of the major indexes, took a major tumble. If you take a month-by-month approach, you will likely see the impact of various events, ranging from 9/11 to the run up to various wars to the economic meltdown of late 2007 and the ensuing Great Recession.

Reduce those charts to the last five years and the latest twelve-month charts. Like anyone who navigates the skies or seas, knowing the territory that has been covered in the past makes one more comfortable to move forward. The problem with investing—and this is as true for the most sophisticated in the financial world as it is for those just starting out—is that there is no accurate forecast as to when the seas might be choppy or the skies filled with storms. That's where Newsvesting can help in moving forward.

Warren Buffett has stressed the need for investors to read everything they can about investing. And that reading is not limited to current information about companies, stocks, bonds, funds, and financial news. It also includes getting up to speed with a general knowledge of modern American history and world history as well. All of this takes time and patience, but so does creating or maintaining a healthy investment portfolio.

STEP 2 IDENTIFYING INVESTMENT-RELATED ISSUES

Just reading the various financial papers, such as the *Wall Street Journal*, and the multitude of cable and online sources, ranging from CNBC, Fox Business News, Newsmax Finance, and Bloomberg Business, it's easy to be overwhelmed with conflicting stories and opinions about virtually everything related to business, finance, and investing. In part that's because of the general nature of modern media. As stated, the secret to most news/talk programs, as well as to most news/business articles, is that their producers/editors require that each segment of a show or most articles show balance. That means someone will be sure of something and someone else will just as confidently disagree. And if the two sides aren't presented in the same show or article, they will surely compete for your attention within a matter of hours or days as separate but distinctly opposing views, leading to confusion as to which way anything from the economy to a given company is headed.

With the added impact of social media, the amount of clutter we all encounter from various media is overwhelming.

But there is a way to cut through and weigh all of that information, and for individual investors it does not require massive computers, PhDs on call, or endless algorithms.

It all starts, as does any legal argument or academic debate, with culling through the evidence to find the issues that matter to you and your approach to gathering that evidence. In short: read, read, read. If you haven't developed that habit yet, now's a great time to begin.

Let's start with the basics. There are must-haves in searching to determine the major issues that confront a Newsvestor. In print or online, publications such as the *Wall Street Journal*, still the crown jewel of daily financial print news, are a basic staple to a Newsvestor, just as the *New York Times* or *Washington Post* is to an academic debater or the compendium of recently reported court cases is to a lawyer in a given jurisdiction. (Even a handicapper of horse races religiously feasts on the facts and figures found in a daily racing form.)

The headlines in each section give an early tip to the stories that will develop in other publications or business news programs as the day goes along.

Critics of Newsvesting will suggest that no layperson can possibly replace the skill of trained financial experts by following headlines in newspapers, business and television news programs, and online sites. That's true in part if you don't seek out a trained professional to assist as your mentor, coach, or professor. But to Newsvest while preparing to seek their added counsel is not only smart but essential.

So the Newsvesting process starts with a dedicated examination of both print and online publications each morning and throughout the day. Many of the more up-to-date online sources come from news networks—both financial and general news-oriented.

STEP 3 CREATING A FLOW CHART

As noted earlier, every debate, argument, or trial can be reduced to a set of issues, arguments, and evidence. That give-and-take can then be reduced to pages on which those issues and their developments can be tracked.

Do an experiment. Take the major headlines from the front pages of the various news, market, and investment sections of the *Wall Street Journal* and paraphrase them into one line each. Before moving to other business sites, visit one conservative/right-leaning online news site (such as DrudgeReport.com) and one liberal/left-leaning site (such as Huffington-post.com) to get a quick feel for what both sides of the political spectrum view to be the day's top headline. It may seemingly have nothing to do with the economy or investing. But if both sites share the same topic as their top headline, write it on your flow sheet as an issue.

Quickly move to other sites, such as the online sites for Fox News and Newsmax on the center-right and CNN and MSNBC to the center-left. Again you will get a sense of the top news issues of the day. As before, focus on those that repeat on numerous sites, even if their stories or viewpoints seem wildly different.

Before going any further, determine what it might take algorithms and PhDs days to determine. That is, ask yourself, "Do any of these stories seem like something that could impact me, my family, my paycheck, or the company I work for in any significant way?" This is the start of learning to discern the impact of news stories on potential or existing investments. As you move along the Newsvesting process, determining the impact of issues and evidence will be increasingly important.

Finally, look at the online versions of the three major broadcast news networks. While these networks often lean in particular directions (mainly center-left), their headlines will confirm the degree to which certain news headlines will dominate the so-called mainstream media for a given day.

If it sounds like you will burn up a few hours of your morning, you will soon learn that not to be the case. After a bit of practice, your flow sheet for each day can be created within thirty or forty-five minutes.

Often the major news stories (politics, wars, trends, etc.) won't be in sync with the major investment news stories. But starting with the *Wall Street Journal* and then briefly running through the more broad news sites, Newsvestors are ready to move to the major financial broadcast and online news sites, such as CNBC, Fox Business, Bloomberg, Newsmax Finance, and Yahoo's finance page.

Again, start by focusing on the major financial news issues they each focus on, flowing only those stories whose general subject matter is reported on at least several of the sites at the same time.

At first your list of issues will seem long and look sloppy and disorganized. And for a time your research will take several hours, which when starting out can be separated into various times of the day. But within a week or two the Newsvestor inside you will emerge, and within a month you'll be a pro at spotting the news and financial themes that dominate the media. Your flow sheet will emerge after less than an hour's work in the morning, and soon you will be able to do quick updates during the day and at night to keep abreast of news trends and the various potential investment-related issues that you intend to follow.

In that first week and into the first month, prioritize your issues by taking stories that are front-page headlines for both general news organizations, such as the broadcast news networks, and the business publications and broadcast sites, and place them at the top of your next day's flow page. Those will be the hot-button issues that will transform one from a novice to a Newsvestor.

As you make your lists, set them out during the morning on a page or spreadsheet, with the issues in the extreme left column. As you gather more information about a topic, write a quick sentence that describes what the news story says, then create a web link or save the story. Now you're starting the process of gathering your evidence, carefully looking for any rules that might be decisive in the future. Examples might include a Federal Reserve decision on interest rates, a future decision by a federal or state agency, an upcoming civil trial impacting a corporation, or the next corporate earnings report.

With your preliminary month's worth of issues and evidence in hand, you're ready to start setting out your investment issues. This is when true Newsvesting begins.

STEP 4 SETTING YOUR ISSUES AND GATHERING EVIDENCE

After a month's worth of listing major news and investment stories and linking stories to them, you should start to have a feel for events at home and around the world. Certain issues will emerge as dominant of the prior month. To decide what issues or themes you think might be worthy of Newsvesting, consider this list of sectors of the equity markets. warning: Do not let the list overwhelm you.

Agriculture	Financial
Banking	Food and Beverage
Basic Materials	Hardware
Capital Goods	Healthcare
Chemicals	Industrial Goods
Clothing	Information Technology (IT)
Conglomerates	Insurance
Communication	Investing
Construction	IT Services
Consumer Durables	Media
Consumer Goods	Medical Facilities
Consumer Nondurables	Metals and Mining
Credit	Real Estate
Drugs	Services
Electronics	Software Transportation
Energy	Technology
Entertainment	Utilities

The list can seem daunting, and there are plenty of sites on the Web that can define each sector in greater detail, but you'll see which topics are the most dominant, which are the most interesting, and which you understand the best. Your sectors of interest will narrow to a handful or slightly more.

As you monitor your issues it will be necessary to start researching the most important part not only of Newsvesting but of all investment decisions: good, solid companies you consider to be the best in the sectors your issues have led you to. And that requires some solid information gathering.

Consider Elbit Systems Ltd., a little-known company to even the most sophisticated investment bankers and stockbrokers. But when talk of a potential U.S.-led nuclear agreement with Iran started to simmer in early January 2015, it became clear that Israeli leaders felt a substantial threat could develop from the deal.

In researching the various technology tools that a nation such as Israel would use to protect itself, Elbit Systems stuck out. The potential Iran nuclear agreement had already become an issue on my flow chart. Elbit was consistently mentioned as a company related to it. Here's how I got to Elbit.

Negotiations between the United States, the United Kingdom, Germany, France, Russia, and China to reach a comprehensive nuclear agreement with Iran, designed to monitor and allegedly deter Iran from developing offensive nuclear arms, had taken many inconclusive turns through most of 2014. Even pro-Israel news sites were stating that Israeli leaders believed the negotiations with Iran would continue for a long time, with little likelihood that an economic embargo by pro-Western powers would end.

But by December 2014 and certainly by January 2015, the situation had changed substantially. The Obama administration was described as having decided to let Iran fight the growing threat of ISIS. And with Israel concerned about the growing influence of Iran through its proxy Hezbollah within Syria, Israel was accused of conducting strikes in Syria in December 2014 and January 2015 against Hezbollah. An Iranian general was reportedly killed in one of those airstrikes.

Things were heating up. Israeli prime minister Benjamin Netanyahu, who was viewed in most press reports as locked in a tight and potentially losing battle for reelection, launched an unabashed crusade to kill any

U.S.-backed agreement with Iran. House Speaker John Boehner issued an invitation for Netanyahu to address a joint session of Congress. It was clear that Israeli leaders were deeply concerned.

By reading news stories about prior Israeli military strikes in areas such as the Gaza Strip, one thing stood out: they used drones as a central part of their efforts. Some quick online research made it clear that Elbit was the major supplier of this kind of weaponry to Israel. Ironically, the best material that validated Elbit's importance came from anti-Israel online news sources. From all that was written, Elbit's name stood out. Clearly Israel valued Elbit.

I had identified a specific company. The next part of the process was to determine if it was a company and a stock worth investing in.

Here's where Newsvesting can take a funny turn. In looking at Elbit Systems, it became clear that at one time the company's revenues had been dependent on sales in the United States. And in most of the news and financial data that could be found, sales to Israel itself were not mentioned. This despite the fact that Elbit was actually an Israeli company. Their sales were growing faster in Asia and Latin America. And they had a diversified set of niche products and services that went beyond drones and included upgrading aircraft systems and providing improvements in fighting cyberwars.

The company appeared to have stock prices that were a good value compared to other companies in the industry, with a price-to-earnings ratio that was more appealing than the industry average. And orders were backing up for Elbit goods and services. Ironically, the Iranian threat that brought me to Elbit had less to do with my deciding if Elbit was a sound investment.

While Newsvesting, I learned that Elbit was of vital importance in specialized niche areas that would be critical in future military and defense strategies. An investment in Elbit Systems Ltd. in early January 2015 cost about $61 a share. Four months later shares were bumping at or near $80 a share.

In creating a flow sheet for Elbit, there was the original issue of the potential Iran treaty. That quickly led to evidence gathering, which pointed to the perceived growing threat to Israel and how it protects itself. That led to news stories that prominently highlighted the use of drones, which quickly led to stories in which Elbit's name became prominent. That put them into play in my Newsvesting portfolio of possibilities. It was time to list the apparent advantages and disadvantages of buying shares in Elbit.

STEP 5 WEIGHING ADVANTAGES AND DISADVANTAGES
AND APPLYING RULES AND ANALYSIS

The advantages to buying Elbit stock included increasing sales, a diversified market, a niche area or areas of business and products, and good financials, which suggested the stock was undervalued. The disadvantages included the fact that the weakness of Israel's currency (the shekel) was contributing to the company's strong performance and a possibility that the real need for Elbit's products would subside, at least temporarily. Next came my analysis and conclusion. In the end came the weighing of the advantages and disadvantages after having gathered evidence and applied the rules:

+ The likelihood of the Iran agreement being adopted (although this was less relevant)
+ The likelihood of continued international instability that required the type of products and services Elbit provided
+ The general rules applying to the company's financial strength and likely growth.

I decided the advantages outweighed the potential disadvantages. And to clinch the decision, Elbit had a near 2% dividend/yield.

Think of the weighing of these advantages and disadvantages as placing individual news stories on a scale of justice. The stories you view as less persuasive, you give less weight to. Those more reasoned or filled with facts that are timely and relevant, you weigh heavier. Sort them with one side going toward favoring an investment and the other going against. Meanwhile, start eying the performance of the stocks you have researched as relevant to your issue. If after a reasonable time the shares of the company or companies you have identified appear to move in relation to the news you have identified with your issue, or if you feel confident they will, take action.

If you are completely unsure, and those scales of advantages and disadvantages seem balanced, then follow the old rule of academic debate or a deadlocked jury: let the presumption go to the status quo and the deadlocked defendant go free. In other words, toss the issue aside, forget a Newsvestment, and move on.

In the instance of Elbit Systems, the advantages far outweighed the disadvantages. The fact that Elbit's back orders for products were approaching $7 billion at the end of 2014 assured a nice stream of revenue and obvious growth. And the instability throughout the world, combined with a rapid growth in technologically advanced areas, such as drones and cybersecurity software, both of which Elbit excelled in, made Elbit Systems a Newsvesting choice.

In the instance of Elbit Systems, once it was picked, the issue to be followed was not the Iran agreement as much as it was Elbit itself, and the various subtopics like the need for drones, cyber warfare systems, and other products offered by Elbit to the rest of the world. Also in Newsvesting, as mentioned, it was clear that the company's strong performance was in part due to the weakness of Israel's currency. So now Elbit, as an actual Newsvestment, would require its own flow chart in which these subissues would need to be monitored.

By late April a new issue arose. The Israeli government was once again seeking to privatize several government-owned corporations, including Israel Military Industries, the eighty-year-old company known for the Uzi submachine gun. Elbit Systems was mentioned as a possible purchaser, either in part or in whole.

That potential investment by Elbit would require watching. Often companies that purchase others see a decline in their stock, at least after any announcement and during any early effort to absorb or integrate the purchased entity. But quick research showed that the Israeli government had attempted privatization efforts before, only to see those efforts blocked by unions. So as my cut-off date for this book arrived, Elbit was still on my active flow chart. And as mentioned, it soared from around $61 a share to nearly $80 in just a matter of months.

MONITORING ISSUES AND KEEPING UP WITH THE FLOW

Once a Newsvestment is chosen, it requires daily monitoring. The first step is to set the chosen company's stock symbol on your handheld device, always available to check. That sounds silly, and certainly in years to come even handhelds will likely be replaced by a more virtual way of keeping track of such information. But Newsvestors who fail to have their investments in sight day and night should not be Newsvesting. Why? The answer is not so they can trade shares every other day or at the slightest dip or rise. That truly is the old day trading of the late 1990s.

But as news and information now moves at a much faster rate, so do the factors that might substantially impact a company and the value of its shares.

Even sudden and swift shifts in value won't usually justify taking action. But make no mistake, while Newsvestors buy shares of a good company to hold for years, they must be prepared to seize opportunities or cut inevitable disastrous losses with confidence. The goal here is to make money and to put that money to work making more. That's the advantage a Newsvestor has over the average investor in an age in which fewer Americans are saving enough and are not receiving enough for their saving efforts to ever feel as comfortable as they head toward retirement as did their parents or the generations that came before them.

Now it's time to look at Newsvesting in action in specific financial segments.

CHAPTER **5**

Obamacare:
In Sickness and Wealth

WHAT'S THE BEST TREATMENT?

Never has the mixture of a little knowledge of recent history in combination with a constant eye on evolving news stories proved to be more valuable than to those who chose to ignore the prevailing news chatter and Newsvesting *with*—not against—Obamacare.

What's that? No way, you cry. After all, the Affordable Care Act (which even President Obama himself finally dubbed Obamacare) is one of the most intrusive and unpopular measures in our nation's history. It created red tape, forced companies to pay for unwanted types of healthcare coverage, and remained unpopular in the polls with a majority of Americans years after its passage.

Yes, that's all true. And it all proves the point that Newsvestors must separate personal political views from the data and information in order to find and hold new investment opportunities that arise as a result of the world of politics and policy.

To understand how President Obama's version of universal healthcare would be received by healthcare providers and to understand who expected to benefit from it required Newsvestors to go back to the days of so-called Hillarycare and 1993–94.

The Week did its homework in a 2015 examination of the involvement of big business and Obamacare during the debate over universal healthcare in the 1990s, which politically damaged the Democrats and helped Newt

Gingrich and his fellow Republicans take control of the U.S. House of Representatives. They point to a *New York Times* story that reported that big health insurers, such as Prudential, Cigna, Aetna, MetLife, and Travelers, parted ways with the Health Insurance Association and their effective "Harry and Louise" ads that killed off the Clinton effort. Instead, those large health insurers chose to create the Coalition for Managed Competition.

The coalition was far more Clinton-healthcare-reform friendly for a reason. Their members knew then what didn't change by 2010. Expanding healthcare coverage to more individuals would mean more money and profits for their companies. Oddly enough, that fact seemed lost on most Americans in 1994 and in 2010 with the passage of Obamacare.

When the battle over passage of Obamacare was raging in early 2010, there seemed to be a perception among much news media and the public that healthcare providers—clinics and hospitals, drug manufacturers, and insurance companies—were passionately against Obamacare. The last thing these private businesses wanted was a government takeover of healthcare, right?

Wrong. In effect, DC wasn't going to take over the business of healthcare; it was mainly going to funnel hundreds of billions of taxpayer dollars mostly to the disadvantaged to allow them to purchase healthcare plans from existing private insurers. (The Congressional Budget Office estimated that 170 million people would have coverage through Medicare, Medicaid, and the Obamacare insurance exchanges by 2023, an increase of about 50% from 2013.) In other words, Obamacare was designed to guarantee tens of millions of new customers to the healthcare industry.

There were three reasons for the widespread misperception that private healthcare providers were opposed to Obamacare. The first was President Obama himself. He publicly and repeatedly denounced the healthcare industry as predatory profiteers that needed to be reined in.

In remarks to a Joint Session of Congress on September 9, 2009, Obama first stated, "There are now more than thirty million Americans who cannot get [health] coverage." He then went on to point out that the insurance companies were to blame for that fact and more.

The president continued:

> But the problem that plagues the healthcare system is not
> just a problem for the uninsured. Those who do have insurance

have never had less security and stability than they do today. More and more Americans worry that if you move, lose your job, or change your job, you'll lose your health insurance too. More and more Americans pay their premiums, only to discover that their insurance company has dropped their coverage when they get sick, or won't pay the full cost of care. It happens every day. . . .

One man from Illinois lost his coverage in the middle of chemotherapy because his insurer found that he hadn't reported gallstones that he didn't even know about. They delayed his treatment, and he died because of it. Another woman from Texas was about to get a double mastectomy when her insurance company canceled her policy because she forgot to declare a case of acne. By the time she had her insurance reinstated, her breast cancer had more than doubled in size. That is heart-breaking, it is wrong, and no one should be treated that way in the United States of America.

The second reason was the relentless attack on healthcare insurance companies by well-funded groups, such as Health Care for America Now (HCAN). Looking back on their early activities after passage of the bill, HCAN patted itself and its supporters on their collective backs.

They proudly proclaimed:

We began the campaign by attacking the insurance industry as the chief villain in the story of America's health insurance crisis. Early local events targeted the industry's trade organization, and HCAN's first major television ad featured a woman who was battling cancer and was willing to take on the insurance companies and the politicians who side with them. This message mobilized the progressive base and moved people in the "middle."

In years past, reformers would chant, "Insure the Uninsured." We won Obamacare with placards that said, "Big Insurance Makes Me Sick" and "It's a crime to deny our care." We campaigned against the insurance industry's stranglehold on our healthcare, which gave them carte blanche to deny coverage and benefits and jack up our rates with impunity. We asked members of Congress whose side they were on—consumers or the insurance companies. We ran television ads that ended with the tagline, "If the insurance companies win, you lose."

The third reason for misperception was the healthcare industry itself. For the most part they offered passive support of Obamacare simply by not launching a public relations campaign against it.

The National Review put it aptly in December 2013:

Indeed, one of the more peculiar aspects of the Obamacare debate has been the mainstream media's apparent bemusement at the insurance industry's support for a law that not only forces people to buy its products (which are necessarily more expensive under the law) but also offers direct taxpayer subsidies to help cover the cost, to the tune of nearly $500 billion over the next ten years.

The healthcare industry spent almost $250 million on lobbying in the first six months of 2013 alone.

Despite some misunderstandings—and perhaps a bit of public relations sleight of hand by some of the industry players—there were reports early on that told Newsvestors what they needed to know, including this report in March 2010 from the *Washington Examiner*:

The Pharmaceutical Researchers and Manufacturers of America—whose $26.1 million lobbying effort in 2009 was the most expensive by any industry lobby in history—hailed the health package as "important and historic."

The second-biggest industry lobby in America, the American Medical Association, also cheered, as did the American Hospital Association, the No. 5 industry lobby.

Even the oft-labeled "bad guy" quietly though publicly gave its support. AHIP (America's Health Insurance Plans), a trade group of big and small health insurance providers, had been instrumental in derailing the

Clinton plan in 1993. Nancy Pelosi was talking about it when she mentioned the "big, bad insurance companies." But as the *Miami Herald* reported in March 2010:

> In November 2008, just days after Obama's landslide victory, America's Health Insurance Plans, a trade group, made a stunning announcement, saying it favored universal coverage and supported a law that would stop insurers from rejecting applicants because of preexisting conditions. "Universal coverage is within reach," the group said in a historic press release. After being adamantly opposed to reform during the Clinton years, AHIP said it had changed its mind—based on one condition: Any reform plan had to require that all individuals have insurance or pay stiff penalties.

It took some media awhile to catch on, but most eventually did. Below is a good, if conservatively biased, summation of the situation from the right-leaning watchdog news service Breitbart.com in March 2012.

> In a nutshell, Obamacare is set up to subsidize health insurance companies as well as hospitals and pharmaceutical companies.
> So aside from a few pesky details, what's not to love about Obamacare if you're an insurance company? With it, there is the promise of a long life on the government dole, with little chance of going out of business.
> The challenge for health insurers was how to partner with President Obama and media in convincing Americans that they were really enemies, struggling for control of healthcare—the private sector vs. the government. Health insurers succeeded by following [this] plan: 1) Passive support for Obamacare with no public relations effort against the law and 2) Allowing President Obama, the Democrats and liberal media to demonize their industry and paint them as "the bad guys," particularly at moments when the law was under attack from Republicans.

Additionally, a Google news search in May 2012 turned up this analysis from the Roosevelt Institute, which points to yet another reason for private insurance companies and others in the healthcare industry to support Obamacare—the alternative to the law might conceivably be single-payer or government-run healthcare:

> The healthcare bill just signed into law entrenches the centrality of private health insurance companies and contains no serious proposals to limit costs.
> The "reform" introduced by this bill largely promotes the status quo by pulling more people into an expensive healthcare system that is managed and funded by private insurers with no countervailing government option.

As time passed and Obamacare became entrenched as the law of the land, even mainstream media outlets like the *New York Times* were reporting the new, cozy relationship between Washington and the insurance industry. Consider a story headlined "Health Care Law Recasts Insurers as Obama Allies" from November 2014:

> Since the Affordable Care Act was enacted in 2010, the relationship between the Obama administration and insurers has evolved into a powerful, mutually beneficial partnership that has been a boon to the nation's largest private health plans and led to a profitable surge in their Medicaid enrollment. . . .
> "Insurers and the government have developed a symbiotic relationship, nurtured by tens of billions of dollars that flow from the federal Treasury to insurers each year," said Michael F. Cannon, director of health policy studies at the libertarian Cato Institute.
> Insurers, often aligned with Republicans in the past, have built their business plans around the law and will strenuously resist Republican efforts to dismantle it. Since Mr. Obama signed the law, share prices for four of the major insurance companies—Aetna, Cigna, Humana and UnitedHealth—have more than doubled, while the Standard & Poor's 500-stock index has increased about 70 percent.

> The Congressional Budget Office estimates that 170 million people will have coverage through Medicare, Medicaid and the insurance exchanges by 2023, an increase of about 50 percent from 2013. . . .
>
> Aetna, in reporting its third-quarter results, said many people thought 2014 would "spell the death of our industry." But, the company said it is having "a very good year," thanks in part to "excellent performance in our government business, which now represents more than 40 percent of our health premiums."

The reason for that "very good year" was summed up in a *Forbes* article headlined "Health Plan Premiums Are Skyrocketing According to New Survey of 148 Insurance Brokers, With Delaware Up 100%, California 53%, Florida 37%, Pennsylvania 28%" in April 2014:

> Health insurance premiums are showing the sharpest increases perhaps ever according to a survey of brokers who sell coverage in the individual and small group market. Morgan Stanley's healthcare analysts conducted the proprietary survey of 148 brokers. The April survey shows the largest acceleration in small and individual group rates in any of the 12 prior quarterly periods when it has been conducted.
>
> The average increases are in excess of 11% in the small group market and 12% in the individual market. Some states show increases 10 to 50 times that amount. The analysts conclude that the "increases are largely due to changes under the ACA."
>
> The analysts conducting the survey attribute the rate increases largely to a combination of four factors set in motion by Obamacare: Commercial underwriting restrictions, the age bands that don't allow insurers to vary premiums between young and old beneficiaries based on the actual costs of providing the coverage, the new excise taxes being levied on insurance plans, and new benefit designs.

Those factors aren't likely to change in the years to come. If anything, they will push premiums and company profits higher.

FEELING ILL THAT YOU MIGHT
HAVE MISSED AN OPPORTUNITY?

One might argue that the 2014 reports about a surge in the value of shares in the largest insurance companies would be of little value to potential investors, since that train, no matter how valuable in hindsight, has already left the station. But to a Newsvestor the likely increase in value for these companies would have been apparent much earlier.

Consider a *Forbes* article a year earlier that proclaimed "ObamaCare Enriches Only the Health Insurance Giants and Their Shareholders." That story, which scrutinized the meteoric rise in value of shares of the largest health insurers, appeared in October 2013. As an example, in that month, shares of Aetna were trading in the $65 range. But even as the big insurers were gaining press for their success on Wall Street, it was clear that two important ingredients would likely be present to spur Aetna and others to even higher values in the future. One was obvious: Obamacare was still expanding the number of mandated insureds. The other required a look at the likely political landscape after the 2014 midterm elections.

It had become vogue in conservative circles to write about the possibility of a potential Republican takeover of the U.S. Senate in 2014, combined with the GOP's likely retention of control in the House, to provide the possibility for a move to repeal the Affordable Care Act. I joined other columnists in engaging in such hopeful possibilities.

But in reality there was never any hope for such a repeal of Obamacare. First, even if Republicans had won every politically possible Senate contest, they would not have the number of votes needed to pass such a repeal and sustain a presidential veto. That rendered the House and its potentially stronger GOP control irrelevant.

That meant that the big health insurers would likely continue to see their revenues, profits, and the value of their shares grow beyond the 2014 election.

And it wasn't just insurance companies that stood to gain by Obamacare, both when it was passed and as it was implemented. As the Huffington Post reported in May 2010: "'[Pharmaceutical companies] came out of this better than anyone else,' said Ramsey Baghdadi, a Washington health policy analyst who projects a $30 billion, 10-year net gain for the industry."

Indeed, despite the public relations games being played by some during the lobbying for, passage of, and continued implementation of Obamacare, the vigilant Newsvestor could have known the truth about Obamacare from the outset by doing what wise investors always do—following the money. Perhaps CNN in March 2010 reported all one needed to know about Obamacare: "The whole package will cost roughly $940 billion over 10 years to provide expanded insurance coverage, according to [the Congressional Budget Office]." Enough said.

The following is a brief glance at the rise in four major healthcare stocks following the passage of the Affordable Health Care Act in March 2010.

PFIZER

Pfizer Inc. is, by revenue, one of the largest pharmaceutical companies in the world. Its stock share price did not trend upward immediately after passage of Obamacare. (Likely investors took Nancy Pelosi at her word: they didn't yet know what was in the bill.)

In any case, Pfizer stock sold at about $18 a share as late as January 2011 before jumping to $21 in May 2011, $24 in July 2012, and $29 in July 2013. By March 2014 it was $32 a share, and by March 2015 it was $35.

AETNA

Aetna is a managed healthcare company that sells health insurance plans and related services. The company is a member of the Fortune 500.

Aetna's share price actually declined in the uncertain investment climate that immediately followed Obamacare becoming law, but soon its stock was on a long ascent. From March 2010 to April 2011, the share price rose at one point from $35 to $42. A year later, in April 2013, the stock sold at $57. By April 2014 it was $71, and by March 2015 the stock was $108 a share!

LIFEPOINT

LifePoint Health Inc. (LPNT) is a hospital company that has more than sixty-five hospitals in twenty-one states and more than $4.5 billion in annual revenues. Its share price followed the path of Aetna. From April 2010 to April 2011, its price rose from $36 to $42. By 2013 it had risen to $53. By April 2014 it was at $57, and by April 2015 it was $78 a share. Trade volume rose concurrently with the price, going from less than one hundred thousand shares traded a day to over a million in just a couple of years.

UNITEDHEALTH GROUP

UnitedHealth Group is a giant in the insurance and managed-care sector, serving more than eighty-five million individuals worldwide, including all fifty states. Revenues in 2010 were $94 billion. Coming in at 14 on the Fortune 500 rankings, in 2014 it had revenues of $130.5 billion, a 38% increase—four years and one Affordable Health Care Act later.

Need I say more? I doubt it. But I will.

With more people covered comes more care. And that fuels the financials of companies creating the necessary products to take care of what ails them. Chances are, you've never heard of these firms. But the numbers in this area are nothing short of staggering. A few examples from the Inc. 5000:

> Crescendo Bioscience: This San Francisco–based molecular diagnostics company founded in 2002 concentrates on "autoimmune and inflammatory diseases such as rheumatoid arthritis." 2010 revenues—$147,810. 2013—$27.3 million, an uptick of 18,375 percent!

> The HCI Group: This Jacksonville, Florida–based company was founded in 2009 as a "specialist in healthcare IT consultancy. The company performs installations for electronic health records, validation, testing, launching, optimization, and ongoing support." It had 2010 revenues of $259,420. By 2013 they were at $34.6 million, up 13,231 percent!

> Alliance Health: Headquartered in Salt Lake City, Alliance Health "operates health condition-specific online social communities, serving more than a million users, that provide support, information, advice, and access to medications and supplies through its pharmacy network." Founded in 2006, its 2010 revenues were $2.4 million. By 2013, they had risen 3,490 percent to $85.6 million.

These just barely scratch the surface. Over three dozen health-related companies on the Inc. list reported over 1,000% gains in the three-year period between 2010 and 2013. Not exactly your run-of-the-mill return on certificates of deposit.

THE COURT'S DIAGNOSIS

Even challenges to the Affordable Care Act provided opportunities for alert Newsvestors to enter what some would consider a frothy healthcare insurer/provider market.

For example, in March 2015 the U.S. Supreme Court heard a second case on Obamacare. Would the justices rule to uphold this five-year-old federal law or would they disallow the massive federal subsidies to the states, which are the heart and soul of the law?

At stake wasn't just the future of Americans' healthcare. Another titanic repercussion of the Court's decision would be critical for Wall Street.

Take, for example, the huge healthcare corporation Hospital Corporation of America (HCA) based in Nashville, Tennessee. Current and potential HCA shareholders locked in on every word coming from the justices' mouths as they heard the case. Of particular interest to investors was a statement by Justice Anthony Kennedy to the effect that a ruling against Obamacare in this case might pose "constitutional problems."

A day later, an article appeared in HCA's hometown newspaper, the *Tennessean*:

> What is a question worth? Try $1.7 billion. That's the impact on the one-day market capitalization of HCA after the King vs. Burwell oral arguments before the U.S. Supreme Court.
>
> After oral arguments . . . HCA stock rose $4.14 per share; with over 420 million shares outstanding, that's a $1.7 billion swing in market capitalization in one day. . . .
>
> In addition to Justice Kennedy, the questioning from Justices Breyer, Ginsburg, Sotomayor and Kagan suggest that four votes are firmly in the camp of sustaining the Obama administration's interpretation of the ACA, i.e. that the tax subsidies are available to both the federal and state exchanges. This means that the federal government needs only one of the remaining five Justices to prevail. The markets' spontaneous interpretation is that the one vote may be Justice Kennedy.

This new development in the continuing saga of Obamacare, even though it was largely speculation about one statement made by a justice, illustrates the power of political events to influence the stock market. Whatever else a fully intact Affordable Care Act might mean to the nation, it meant money, and lots of it, for the right players in the healthcare industry.

Conventional wisdom and political prevailing winds pointed toward the carefully contrived perception that big health insurance companies and their tangential remora would be vehemently opposed to anything that smacked of a government takeover of their industry. After all, they had the most to lose, didn't they?

Far from it. Turns out the private healthcare industry as a whole, and those who invested in the real news—Newsvesting *with* not *against* Obamacare—had the most to gain.

As for my own Newsvesting on this issue, I chose to ride Aetna (AET). I did so first in very small portions early on, and then purchased substantially more after analysts decided to read into the Supreme Court's questions in the *King v. Burwell* case. But applying a rule that is known well beyond the legal world—that being that only a fool tries to second-guess the Supreme Court—on May 27, 2015, I sold my larger Aetna holdings that had been purchased on March 26 of that same year at an increase in value of around 7%. Yes, it was a short-term gain. But it was achieved in roughly two months!

Aetna would still be around after the Court ruled on a critical aspect of Obamacare. But it was better to let the judicial tea-leaf readers stick around for that decision.

CHAPTER 6

What Light Through Yon Window Breaks?

IT JUST MIGHT BE
A SIGN OF THE TIMES

No economic rumblings in at least a generation have jolted the U.S. economy like the Great Recession from December 2007 until June 2009. And no aspect of that recession was as consequential as the implosion of the residential real estate market.

Looking back, the oncoming destruction of the land bubble and the ensuing mega-crisis in the financial world was perhaps easier to predict than some might suggest.

We all know that trends in America often grow quickly and without much notice. The jaw-dropping run-up in the housing market, which reached full steam by late 1999, seemed to have no downside. In many of the more attractive, upscale markets, older homes were selling at a premium, if only for the right to tear them down and build newer and grander ones. The condo market was hot again, with players such as Donald Trump licensing their names to projects in Sunbelt cities, where the move toward luxury-in-the-sky living was gaining traction.

And the ability to obtain a mortgage had become a given, as institutions gave winks and nods to the requirements necessary to qualify for such loans, while applicants played a bit fast and loose with information about their financial situation.

Affordability wasn't a big deal. The value of real estate just kept going up. In June 2005, *The Economist* led a report with this observation: "NEVER before have real house prices risen so fast, for so long. . . . America has seen one of the biggest increases in house-price inflation over the past year, with the average price of homes jumping by 12.5% in the year to the first quarter. In California, Florida, Nevada, Hawaii, Maryland and Washington, DC, they soared by more then 20%."

The same article reported that a substantial number of homes were being bought as an investment or as second homes. "Flippers buy and sell new properties even before they are built in the hope of a large gain. In Miami, as many as half of the original buyers resell new apartments in this way. Many properties change hands two or three times before somebody finally moves in." Riskier interest-only mortgages, "negative amortization loans," and ARMs were the rule rather than the exception.

But while alarms were being sounded, interest rates remained low and lending institutions kept feeding an insatiable house-hungry populace.

Sometimes Newsvesting requires not just looking to large national or global media sources. There are occasions when the media net needs to be widened to include large metropolitan areas and their local news sources or resort locations that might give an early indication that good times are coming to an end.

In rare instances, your eyes and ears will tell you something you either didn't know or at least did not recognize as important. As mentioned earlier, my own introduction to Newsvesting came in the one story from my weekly national column about the oncoming housing collapse written in early 2006. It was simply a matter of luck that right before I penned the column I had been traveling through South Florida and noticed an odd thing about the Miami skyline. Numerous high-rise buildings seemed topped out and, at first glance, occupied. But each window of each building had the same round light, sort of like on an ultra-large Christmas tree ornament, hanging in the center of the window.

I asked my driver, and he said that these were high-end condominiums or other residential towers where the structures had risen but developers had either run out of capital or failed to attract buyers or both. The local government required the lights so as to avoid the empty structures appearing as a blight on the night skyline.

I had no idea if the story was true, but it caused me to do plenty of research about home and condo sales as well as real estate developments in areas that seemed to be on fire with sales and growth. From that point on, the number of stories about housing markets falling apart just kept on mounting.

We now know that from the apex of that first quarter of 2006, U.S. households lost over $7 trillion in home equity. (The decline preceded— and probably helped cause—the recession itself.) It's estimated that nearly one in four U.S. homeowners with mortgages at some point during or after the recession had outstanding mortgage balances that exceeded the value of their homes. That means they could not sell their homes at a profit, even if there were buyers with ready money.

Residential private investment (mainly housing) fell from its 2006 pre-crisis peak of $800 billion to $400 billion by mid-2009 and largely remained depressed at that level into 2015. Housing prices fell about 30% on average from their mid-2006 peak to mid-2009 and remained at about that level well into 2013.

Among all this bad news there seemed to hang in the back of America's collective mind the presumption that the housing crash had to be coming to a halt soon, given the history of housing declines, and considering that the Great Recession was declared to be over in 2009. But no such robust rebound was on the way—even into 2015. Consider the following weigh-ins from the media.

In the fall of 2010, Bloomberg reported, "Sales of existing houses plunged by a record 27% in July. . . . Demand for single-family houses dropped to a 15-year low and the number of homes on the market swelled."

In January 2011, NBC reported, "Homeownership is falling at an alarming pace, despite the fact that home prices have fallen, affordability is much improved and inventories of new and existing homes are still running quite high."

Bloomberg in April 2012 noted, "Builders began work on fewer homes than forecast in March, signaling a sustained industry recovery will take time to get underway."

That "time to get underway" for a sustained housing recovery dragged on into 2013. In April of that year, CNN reported on "3 reasons the housing recovery may not last" (namely, the housing recovery is being led by investors, the economic recovery is just not strong enough yet, and government cuts will hurt homeowners).

More than a year later, in September 2014, Reuters reported, "The [housing] recovery . . . will likely remain gradual against a backdrop of relatively high unemployment and sluggish wage growth, which are sidelining first-time buyers and keeping many young adults from seeking their own accommodation."

And on it went into 2015, when in January the Associated Press reported on the still-sluggish housing recovery: "U.S. home prices rose at a modest pace in November, held back by weaker sales and a limited number of available houses."

SO WHY NO STICKS AND BRICKS?

There is more than one reason for the excruciatingly slow recovery of the housing market, but prominent among them seemed to be the federal Dodd-Frank Act of 2010, which became law in the wake of the recession that saw as many as five million people lose their homes. Dodd-Frank so heavily regulates banks that it has become doubly difficult for prospective homeowners to qualify for a mortgage, even with sustained low interest rates working in their favor. Another, hidden reason for the sluggishness in home sales is a slowing of the foreclosure process rather than simply more wealth on the part of borrowers. Impaired credit scores are also a factor.

At the heart of this unhappy phenomenon are the millennials, the buzzword that defines the current generation of young adults. Depending on whose definition you subscribe to, millennials are roughly between the ages of eighteen and thirty-five. They are contrasted with the generations preceding them, the baby boomers and Generation X. Basically, millennials means young adults.

While plenty of middle-aged and even senior Americans during the Great Recession and its aftermath had great trouble buying or maintaining a home, it's the millennials whose housing travails chiefly dictated the economics of renting versus ownership. This is no mystery: millennials are at the age when many or most Americans traditionally have purchased a place of their own. But they weren't buying.

There were numerous reasons for this critical group's failure to opt in to the housing market in the same manner their parents and grandparents did.

For starters, college graduates hold record amounts of student debt.

Two out of three recent graduates owed an average debt of about $27,000. As recently as the 1990s, roughly half of all graduates who had student debt averaged a burden of roughly $15,000. According to the Federal Reserve, almost thirty-seven million Americans had student loan debt by 2015. Moreover, at least 60% of that debt was held by people over thirty years old, and 15% was held by those over fifty.

This burden on millennials was compounded by the Great Recession. Many of them were just entering the workforce when the economy took a nosedive. As a result, millennials faced higher rates of poverty and unemployment than the two preceding generations. That was especially true for those with only a high school degree.

Importantly, other changes in American society that affect home-buying are largely independent of the state of the economy. Globalization and rapid technological change not only made undergraduate and advanced degrees more important than ever, but they also created a working world in which lifelong or decades-long careers with a single company were increasingly rare. This made for a dynamic in which millennials and others were hesitant to buy homes for fear they would soon have to sell them and relocate. And millennials were slow to marry, usually waiting until their early or late thirties, if not later.

The disappearance of middle-class jobs has also been a factor. Routine jobs can now be automated. Manufacturing jobs that once allowed many to buy homes and raise families continue to fly across borders or overseas. That leaves low-end jobs that are hard to automate but don't pay a lot.

Much of the millennials' hesitation to buy real estate was summed up by Mark Colwell of the Redfin Research Center:

> Many Millennials delay these major life events [like home ownership], focusing instead on building their careers and enjoying their limited free time with their like-minded friends in the city. Millennials who flock straight from college to . . . expensive cities are making a choice to spend their income on quadruple-digit rents and eight-dollar gourmet hot dogs from trendy food trucks. This means they're not saving for a down payment, further removing them from the housing market.

Even by 2015 many millennials were finding justification for their unwillingness to buy homes. Yale University Professor Robert Shiller, the creator of the noted S&P Case-Shiller Housing Index, found that housing prices did not outperform inflation over a one-hundred-year period. In other words, buying a home was no longer necessarily a good long-term investment.

Also, many of the existing home sales in many parts of the country had been purchases of pricey homes, the buyers of which could more easily qualify for mortgages than could millennials and others.

Finally, a number of millennials seemed hesitant to make big financial commitments for fear there will be little if any retirement money for them through Social Security or other government programs, according to Pew Research.

The point to the Newsvestor was that even if the U.S. economy became fully robust again (a fact that has been heartedly proclaimed since 2012 to the present), a lot of millennials will likely stay out of the housing market, or, at least, further delay their entry. The economic recovery following the Great Recession was not a recovery that suggested a major shift any time soon away from the trend toward renting apartments and other properties. Moreover, the millennials told us in survey after survey that many, if not most of them, were still partial to renting over buying. It was a continuing trend that showed few signs of slowing down significantly.

Until public opinion surveys show that the percentage of millennials who want to own a home match up with the percentage who say they feel they are ready and able to own a home, companies that own and manage higher-end apartments, as well as the strip centers that feed off of them, will probably be an area to consider for investment purposes.

For those working off their own intuition—or faulty information—this slow economic recovery almost six years after the Great Recession ended may have been as surprising as it was frustrating. But to prospective homebuyers and other investors who were carefully monitoring the media, the signs have been there all along that the U.S. housing market still hasn't righted itself.

For example, many potential homebuyers compulsively monitor interest rates to see when buying a home makes the most sense. But upon studying the issue, many come to the sensible conclusion that fluctuating interest rates are not such a reliable guide for deciding when to buy. For one thing, it's generally true that when interest rates increase, the economy is improving. And if the economy is getting better, then housing prices usually trend upward. So often these two factors can cancel out each other.

Moreover, predicting the rise and fall of interest rates can be a fool's errand. In early 2015, some experts said rates were bound to rise, others said they wouldn't, and still others said any increase would be small. "There is no rush to buy for the interest rates because we don't see rates moving very quickly or very much from this year to next," said Nela Richardson, chief economist for Redfin Research, in an interview with *U.S. News & World Report.* "The housing market is not one where anyone should feel an urgency to buy now."

And in April 2014, *OC Housing* reported, "Manipulating . . . interest rates can only carry the market so far."

SO WHAT SHOULD
A NEWSVESTOR LOOK FOR?

The most sensible and reliable concept to monitor for housing trends is the U.S. economy in general: employment, income, wages, and so on. Since the Great Recession supposedly ended in June 2009, a Google search on some of these topics would have yielded reams of information that indicated that economic recovery had been excruciatingly slow or even nonexistent.

Take employment, for example. In June 2009, MarketWatch reported that when those forced to take part-time jobs instead of full-time jobs were added to those who had given up their search for a job, the actual rate of those not working was more than 16%, or more than double the rate it had been just a few years ago. That number had not diminished greatly into 2015.

Or take the public's mood. CNBC reported in the summer of 2011, "More Americans Think the Economy Will Never Recover." Does that sound like a public that was in the mood to make a thirty-year commitment to buying a house?

A year later, in June 2012, *The Economist* quoted from a summary of the global financial system by the Bank for International Settlements: "The world is now five years on from the outbreak of the financial crisis, yet the global economy is still unbalanced and seemingly becoming more so as interacting weaknesses continue to amplify each other." Again, no end in sight to the world's economic malaise.

Ditto in the summer of 2013, said UCLA economist Edward Leamer. The economic recovery is "not a recovery. It's not even normal growth. It's bad."

By mid-2014, some projections of economic growth were improving, but reality still wasn't justifying any cautious optimism. CNBC ran the headline, "Bad to worse: US economy shrank more than expected."

And as late as February 2015, Gallup CEO Jim Clifton told Fox News, "The number of full-time jobs . . . as a percent of the total population is the lowest it's ever been."

A Google or Yahoo search on "wages" revealed in January 2015, "Once you look at inflation, which has been around two percent, inflation-adjusted wage growth has been around zero for the last five years," said Elise Gould of the Economic Policy Institute.

A final note on the careful monitoring of housing and real estate fundamentals on Web searches: sometimes a more complex term can tell you what's key to real estate investment or to real estate investment trusts. Consider the often-mentioned "quantitative easing."

Most have a good idea of what it is now. But when we first started hearing about it years ago, many needed a more substantial definition of what came to be known as QE. The quick definition is "an unconventional monetary policy in which a central bank purchases government securities or other securities from the market in order to lower interest rates and increase the money supply. Quantitative easing increases the money supply by flooding financial institutions with capital in an effort to promote increased lending and liquidity."

Technically, quantitative easing does not involve the U.S. government printing more dollars. In practice, however, it serves the same purpose: to prime a weak economy.

For investors, what was important to remember is that if there was an economic policy of quantitative easing going on, then they could bet the economy was hurting and that little or nothing else was working to stand things right again. And that meant millennials and others still thought about renting property instead of buying it.

Or as *Investors Business Daily* put it in January 2015, the "home ownership rate continues to dive, wiping out the gains from the housing boom [before the Great Recession]. Many Americans have nothing to show for federal policies [designed to boost] home ownership."

In March 2015, CBNC reported that an old problem from the recession was resurfacing:

> After the worst national housing crash in history, the picture of distress continues to improve, but now with one worrisome aberration. For the first time in more than two years, the number of repeat foreclosures took a U-turn and was higher in January compared to a year ago.
>
> New repeat foreclosures rose 11 percent in January from December and accounted for more than half of all new foreclosures, according to Black Knight Financial Services.

Armed with all of those news stories and numerous opinion surveys suggesting that too many people either were in no mood or no condition to be buying a new or existing home, what was a Newsvestor to do?

It probably was a no-brainer to turn to investment vehicles related to apartments and residential rentals as it became clear that people were losing their homes left and right and the housing market was in the tank. But by the start of 2014 the flow of news alerts had already started to jab at an expected return to the happy days of another national land grab, with both existing and new housing taking off like a rocket.

There was just one problem. Too many of those stories had caveats or terms like "starting to see," and few sounded resolute about a true rebound of the housing market. At the same time, opinion reports on millennials and their attitudes about home purchases were starting to reach a critical mass. Investors had to answer the simple question: Do I think the housing market will roar back this year or do I put my money on a continued trend of growth in rental housing and apartments?

Looking at all of the stories, Newsvestors would have started a serious search for investment opportunities in the rental side of the housing equation.

Being relatively simple in terms of investment strategies and how to implement them, Newsvestors could have looked at publicly held companies that occupied this space and made a choice to make a series of investments in both low, medium, and large cap companies with a mind that at some point the housing market would indeed begin to grow, but that, given the weight of housing news coupled with opinion research among the youngest of potential homeowners, any investment in a solid company that offered a publicly held real estate investment trust (REIT) could likely be counted on to produce a reasonable long-term (being held for more than a year) gain when sold, and in some cases, a nice little income component as well.

On the smaller cap side a look at Preferred Apartment Communities in late 2013 provided the perfect low-cost entry into the publicly traded REIT arena. After having founded the much larger Post Properties years earlier, John Williams emerged from a scorched real estate market after the Great Recession with a track record of success in the area of high-end rental and commercial properties.

Williams's departure from Post Properties was an unhappy one, and by some accounts, it was a story of greed and disloyalty on the part of others he had helped lead to personal wealth and corporate success.

Starting another publicly held version of Post was no easy thing, but by 2014 Preferred Apartments (APTS) was holding strong for a small-cap company. In January 2014, APTS was selling at around $8 a share and company shares were trading in a relatively tight range.

For Newsvestors reading between the headlines, that suggested that the much-heralded boom in home sales, both new and existing, was not materializing. It was clear that most publicly traded companies in the residential rental space were headed for water that would lift all boats.

But what made Preferred Apartments more attractive was the strong dividend/yield of nearly 7%. Few analysts were following the company, but the few who did had either strong buy or buy positions on the stock. And they were right.

By early 2015, shares of APTS had climbed to over $10 a share and continued to hold its consistent payment of dividends. To Newsvestors, Preferred Apartments was an ideal way to ride the wave of news at a cheap price and with good quarterly income to boot. Yes, the stock was thinly traded, thus making it more vulnerable in rough times. But Newsvestors would have known by early 2014 that the demand for residential real estate and the high-end strip malls that often accompanies it would continue to rise.

What the weight of search engine news alerts told Newsvestors more than a year earlier was finally delivered via the gold standard of the *Wall Street Journal* on February 9, 2015, with a story titled "Shift to Renting Won't

Let Up." Not only had the shift of Americans away from the suburbs and back to the cities continued, but the *WSJ* story revealed that a major study by New York University's Furman Center showed that renters were making up more and more of that population.

The article stated, "A resulting demand for apartments is rising so fast that it is starting to overwhelm supply in many cities, which is pushing up housing costs nationwide." The story noted in many cases "long-term demographic trends and changing attitudes have diminished the appeal of the traditional American dream of homeownership."

Boom! Newsvestors who followed the weight of news stories and public opinion were reaping their reward by the time that story made others start to validate the reality of the wave. Preferred Apartments was up by 25% over a twelve-month period. And this small-cap jewel was not alone.

Associated Estates Corporation (AEC) has been around for decades, starting as a family-owned business established to build, manage, and own commercial real estate in the Cleveland suburbs. In the late 1990s, it expanded into other midwestern areas by acquiring apartment communities in Columbus, Indianapolis, Pittsburgh, and Michigan. Via acquisition, the company then expanded into the mid-Atlantic, southeast, southwest, and western regions of the country. By 2010, Associated Estates had become one of only two apartment REITs to achieve positive revenue growth for the year. Its stock was priced at $15.29.

By 2012, Same Community revenue increased by 6% over 2011, while Same Community NOI grew by 6.9%. In addition, the company achieved investment grade rating. Stock price? $16.12.

In April 2015, Associated Estates' portfolio consisted of fifty-six apartment communities containing fifteen thousand units in ten states. And the stock price had soared to $28.50.

Consider also the success of other submarket REITs. From millennials to seniors, people accumulate stuff, and stuff needs a place to stay. Whether it's the former accumulating items for a future house purchase or the latter downsizing but not yet ready to part with sentimental treasures, the outlook for public self-storage REITs has looked bright for years.

You've probably seen one of the twenty-two hundred Public Storage facilities somewhere in the country (or even in Europe). Started in 1972, Public Storage (PSA) is now one of the largest landlords in the world, based on number of tenants. And its stock price, especially in the last five or six years, has given credence to its success in taking care of stuff.

In April 2010, shares of PSA were trading around $95. Two years later, they were around $140. And by April 2015, investors from 2010 had seen their shares more than double to over $194.

THE TROPICS ARE SO NICE
AT THIS TIME OF YEAR

Newsvestors might also reasonably deduce that if millennials aren't spending money on house buying, they must be putting their dollars to use elsewhere. Indeed they are.

One big industry seeing a millennial uptick? Travel. Steve Cohen, vice president of MMGY Global (the largest integrated marketing firm in travel), observed: "Six in ten Millennials would rather spend their money on experiences than material things. This is presumably one of the reasons we've observed the spike in their intentions with respect to leisure travel in the year ahead. The implications for destination and travel-service marketers are quite profound, as Millennials' planning, booking and sharing habits are significantly different from those of older leisure travelers."

In July 2014, Skift travel reporter Dennis Schaal commented: "A half dozen travel companies, including Southwest, Delta, United Continental, Wynn Resorts, Marriott and the Priceline Group have seen fairly massive— more than 50% gains—in their market caps compared with this time last year, as the big keep getting bigger. Hotels dominate the world's 15 largest publicly traded travel companies."

DON'T GIVE UP
ON BASEMENTS AND PORCHES

Dodd-Frank continues to keep lenders playing their cards close to their collective vests. But that doesn't mean there aren't opportunities available.

As the spring of 2015 started to turn to summer, the housing market news remained mixed. Consider this published analysis after a May 2015 report showed that existing home sales for the prior month had fallen 3.3 percent, missing an expected 1 percent gain to 5.24 million units. And earlier that month, home builder sentiment had also fallen.

At the same time, however, reports on housing starts for April 2015 had come in much better than expected. Michael Baele, managing director for private client research at U.S. Bank, noted, "We think the housing market is set for a prolonged period of moderate improvement but not rapid acceleration."

And that basically summed up the way my flow sheet had developed by that time. There was plenty of evidence that the housing market in America was finally picking up and getting hotter. But I continued to list many stories that suggested that rental property would remain strong as well. News stories about weak increases in wages and the low inventory of existing houses to sell balanced it all out for me.

Out of full disclosure, I purchased Preferred Apartment Communities (APTS) in part because I had known John Williams for years, and he headed APTS. Williams and I had a business relationship in completely different areas, but I knew one thing: he was tops in upscale apartments and related ventures.

The stock could have been a risk (given how thinly it was traded), and I had absolutely no help in understanding where it was headed. But with my investment advisor helping me to evaluate it dispassionately, we started purchasing it before it had crossed the $8 level and continued to add bits and pieces over time. By late April, the stock had crossed over the $11 mark, and I decided to sell a large portion of the shares at a nice profit. All the while I enjoyed its strong dividend/yield. My total profit was well over 25 percent when everything was averaged out.

I knew I would likely be back if the stock declined on an unrelated dip in the market. But it was pretty clear that upscale rental was not going to decline anytime in the nearer future.

Also as part of a long-term strategy, I Newsvested in strong home-builders. My main choice was Lennar (LEN). The company is a home builder, a provider of real estate–related financial services, and a commercial real estate investment, investment management, and finance company. Its shares had increased over 8 percent in the first half of 2015 by the time the news hit that home building was up.

Lennar was a leader in the home-building arena and had strong financial numbers. Most analysts had rated it either a hold or a buy. It wasn't a stock that this Newsvestor felt was worthy of a major investment, given the drift, not surge, in the sales of new houses. But if the economy and the market could stay on the tepid but even course it had charted through most of the first half of the year, it would be another logical one to add to my Newsvesting portfolio.

The bigger play, and one I felt better about for the long term, was Home Depot (HD). With more properties being built for the rental market and low inventory of existing homes for sale in many markets, it figured that Home Depot would be a busy place regardless of what the various housing reports after the first quarter of 2014 might be. It was pretty clear that in late 2014, although the housing market was not on fire in many parts of the nation, plenty of new residential developments were springing up around the nation.

Home Depot's shares were trading at around $105 in late 2014, and by March 2015 they were trading at $117. With its dividend/yield of 2.10 percent and news of a strong first quarter, it seemed that this source of everything building related was a logical choice to hold. Yes, if interest rates rose later in 2015 or 2016, then whatever heat up in home building we were seeing could cool. But Home Depot survived the housing collapse and the Great Recession. Moreover, its chief competitor, Lowes, appeared to be in disarray.

And in Newsvesting, it was clear that "household formation" was really more important to business at Home Depot than whether it resulted in more rentals, sales of existing homes, or new homes being built.

Jim Cramer of CNBC fame noted in the early half of 2015:

> Unfortunately population growth, both from new households and from an immigration standpoint, has been a problem ever since the great recession. The one person openly talking about this issue was Carol Tome, CFO of Home Depot, when she placed it as the core context of consumer spending for her company. Once the great recession started, household formation numbers dropped dramatically to about 500,000 new homes a year from approximately 1.3 million. However, now things seem to be back on track. Home Depot just confirmed a household formation figure of more than 1 million homes. As a result, the Home Depot CFO said she expects to see a dramatic increase in growth for the company.

But when it came to home builders or companies in the residential rental or retail sector, just as was the case leading up to 2006, it was smart to keep a keen eye on things. In the housing industry, Newsvestors won't wait for the mainstream reports to surface. The best rule of thumb I use and rely on is that when everywhere you look a new house or development is going up, it's probably time to start thinking about moving money elsewhere. In other words, do the research and look for signs, even when they look like Christmas ornaments, like the locally mandated ones I saw in those abandoned high-rise condos of South Florida back in 2006!

ISSUE 3 2013-14 Housing Market False Recovery/ Increase in Rental Property—REITS

INITIAL EVIDENCE

April 2013, CNN: "3 reasons the housing recovery may not last."

EXTENDED EVIDENCE

September 2014, Reuters: "Housing recovery will likely remain gradual (due to) high unemployment, sluggish wages sidelining first-time buyers."

January 2015, Investors Business Daily: "Home ownership continues to dive . . . wiping out gains from housing boom before Great Recession."

February 2015, Fox News: "Gallup CEO . . . number of full-time jobs as percentage of population lowest it's ever been."

February 2015, *WSJ*: "Shift to Renting Won't Let Up . . . demand for apartments rising so fast . . . starting to overwhelm supply in many cities."

ISSUE 4 Emerging New Housing Market/ Surge in Home Improvement

INITIAL EVIDENCE

April 2015, U.S. Bank: "Housing market set for prolonged period of improvement . . . but not with rapid acceleration."

EXTENDED EVIDENCE

Spring 2015, Jim Cramer, CNBC: "Carol Tome of Home Depot reports household formations are coming back from huge drop during Great Recession."

ISSUE 3 2013-14 Housing Market False Recovery/ Increase in Rental Property—REITS

ANALYSIS

Strong REITS with significant dividend/yield on the rise in 2014. Mortgages difficult in 2014 for many. Younger buyers still searching higher-end rentals, as are baby boomers sizing down. Search for companies with strong financials, dividends where possible, and who understand higher-end rental or related REIT markets. Even if for the short term, they will go if economy, employment, and wages fail to pick up.

CONCLUSION/ACTION

Purchase Preferred Apartment Communities (APTS) in early 2014, continue purchasing throughout 2014 ($8-$9 range). Also would purchase Associated Estates (AEC); Post Properties (PPS); Public Storage (PSA).

RESULT

Sell 90 percent plus APTS holdings at around $11 a share with a total gain of 25 percent. Prepare to purchase again on overall dips in market.

ISSUE 4 Emerging New Housing Market/ Surge in Home Improvement

ANALYSIS

While housing recovery seemed tepid, it was a recovery. Regardless, expenditures for home improvement would continue to grow with household formation increase.

CONCLUSION/ACTION

Search for publicly traded home builders with strong financials. Lennar (LEN) is quick riser with strong numbers. Purchase in May 2015 at $46.50 per share. Also purchase strongest home improvement/builder supply store, Home Depot, as pick for longer hold.

RESULT

Sell LEN three months later for $52 a share. Hold Home Depot, purchased at $109. Long-term hold with price rising through summer of 2015.

CHAPTER **7**

A Bang-Up Way to Newsvest

IT'S WORTH A SHOT

Conventional wisdom and even the normal flow of news often requires a more circumspect approach. That was certainly the case with Barack Obama and his seemingly less-than-friendly view of the use of military force during his administration.

While it is more than true that the president was set on reducing the U.S. military presence in Iraq and Afghanistan, and his overall approach to military spending was that of cutbacks, the Obama administration was actually the best thing that could have happened to defense contractors and their stock values.

Consider that the administration's reaction to the so-called Arab Spring (which began a series of regime changes in the Middle East) was followed by Obama's adamant desire to reach a nuclear agreement with Iran in his second term. Add to that tepid reactions to other nations that could pose a threat to U.S. security, and it's easy to understand why columnist Victor Davis Hanson, writing in the *Weekly Standard,* labeled Obama, not in a flattering way, the "empire builder."

With respect to the Arab Spring, Hanson wrote: "The new terrorist Islamic State has grandiose schemes of recreating the medieval pan-Arab caliphate. After carving off much of Syria and Iraq for their new theocracy, the jihadists plan to topple the rich Gulf sheikhdoms and grab the holy cities of Mecca and Medina. The Islamic State grew out of two laxities. First, no Western power tried to organize a non-Islamist alternative to the bloody pro-Iranian, pro-Hezbollah Syrian dictatorship of Bashar al-Assad, which was on the verge of falling during the Arab Spring four years ago; instead, Western nations may well have ended up arming and abetting ISIS thugs. Second, for the price of a cheap 2012 reelection talking point, the U.S. fled from Iraq in 2011."

The chaos that resulted in the region led to a huge ramp up in arms and defense-related purchases by various nations in the Middle East. And the Obama administration's push for a nuclear arms agreement with Iran—one that was roundly viewed as one-sided and favorable to Iran at the expense of U.S. allies such as Saudi Arabia and Israel—resulted in more empire building, as Hanson explained:

> The Iranian theocracy fancies itself the reincarnation of the ancient Persian Empire of Cyrus and Xerxes. A soon-to-be nuclear Iran, through its operatives, now controls portions of Syria, Iraq, Lebanon, and, soon, Yemen—and dreams of overturning the Sunni sheikhdoms in the Gulf. . . . I think the administration's policy toward the new Iranian Empire is something like, "They probably won't get the bomb until 2017."

While Hanson's observations may seem exaggerated, they obviously were similar to the thinking of Israel's and Saudi Arabia's leaders, among others in the region. But before examining how Newsvestors have approached the chaos that resulted after the first Arab Spring and later with the Obama push for a nuclear agreement with Iran, it's important to look at the general relationship between modern-day wars, armed conflicts, and defense-related investments.

BULLETS, BOMBS, BUCKS

It's common sense to equate wars and armed conflicts involving America with rising stock prices for defense contractors. There is indeed a correlation, although it's not always exact. In this broader sense it is the job of Newsvestors to monitor geopolitical news and to connect the dots. A key investment strategy is to track the stocks of a few major defense companies in times of war and, importantly, of potential war. An examination of the stock prices of Raytheon, Northrop Grumman, and Lockheed Martin during the wars and rumors of wars of the last generation would have been instructive.

Operation Desert Storm, the 1991 Iraq War, lasted less than six weeks. Ten days before it started, Raytheon stocks were worth $67 a share (and for historical purposes the adjusted price was around $8). A month after the fighting ended, the price had soared to $83 (around $11 as historically adjusted for splits in the stock and dividends). It dropped to $77 ($10 adjusted) by October 1991, and then settled in for a long climb that eventually brought share prices to $105 by September 2014 and $113 by March 2015.

The lesson for Newsvestors? Short wars can lead to short-term opportunities for profit, but the wisest investment in major defense stocks might be over the long haul. Over time, perhaps oddly, defense stocks are often somewhat correlated to the Dow or the S&P 500. But regardless of pullbacks in their price, they always come roaring back.

The Iraq War of 2003–11 is case in point. On March 19, 2003, the day the U.S. invasion got underway, Northrop Grumman share prices stood at $87 ($29 adjusted). Less than two months later, on May 13, two weeks after the invasion was over, the price had hiked to nearly $92 ($30.67 adjusted). As with the Raytheon stocks during and after the 1991 war, share prices dropped moderately once the invasion excitement had died down, then settled into a long ascent. By February 2015 share prices were $167 adjusted.

While these adjusted prices can be confusing, they are critical to understanding, from a historical perspective, the stock's growth in value. To put it bluntly, given the choice of investing in guns or butter for the long term, the modern version of guns might be the safest bet. But for the moment, I'll dispense with these historical adjusted interludes.

News media during these episodes of war were awash with headlines and stories about the conflicts. Newsvestors could have inferred new defense contracts for major contractors from all the war news, and in the months and years following the fighting, there were assorted stories specifically about the need for new defense spending.

Just one example is a *Wall Street Journal* report from September 2011 headlined "Geriatric U.S. Arsenal Needs Expensive Facelift." The article stated:

> The U.S. military is aging, and fast. Air Force planes, on average, are the oldest in the history of that branch of the armed forces, which was founded in 1947, according to the Center for Strategic and Budgetary Assessments, a Washington think

tank with close ties to the Pentagon. The Air Force says the average age of F-15 C and D models, which make up about half of the fleet, is 25 years. That's sprightly compared with the average age of the service's strategic bombers, 34, and refueling aircraft, 47.

Planned retirements mean the Navy has fewer ships today than it had on Sept. 11, 2001—284 now, 316 then. The USS *Enterprise*, the Navy's oldest nuclear-powered aircraft carrier, was commissioned in 1961; an estimated 250,000 sailors have served on the ship during its five-decade career. Deactivating the *Enterprise*, which is scheduled for 2013, will be complex and expensive, Navy officials have said.

Some of the old equipment, battered by warfare, needs to be repaired or replaced. Other vehicles and ships need complete overhauls using up-to-date electronics and other innards. And some especially old models, such as the Air Force's Vietnam-era Huey helicopter, need to be phased out altogether.

Small wars are another feature of the modern geopolitical and investment landscape. You can't get much shorter than the U.S. bombing of Serbia in 1999; it lasted one day. Yet even this brief (and successful) military episode served to jump-start key defense stocks.

Raytheon provides a good example. On March 24, the day of the U.S. bombing, Raytheon stocks finished at $57. Less than two months later, on May 19, the price was $73. Newsvestors would have taken their cue from a headline like this stark one from the BBC on March 24: "NATO Bombs Serbia."

Similar scenarios of suddenly rising defense stock prices happened before, during, and after short armed conflicts involving the United States, most of which are now mostly forgotten: the December 1998 bombing of Iraq and the March 2011 bombing strike on Libya, for example.

More recently a combination of actual and potential wars and episodes of armed conflicts served to propel defense stocks to record highs. From mid-February 2013 to exactly two years later, Raytheon stocks exploded from $54 a share to $107. In the same time span, Lockheed Martin stocks more than doubled in worth, from $88 to $198. And Northrop Grumman shares climbed from $66 to $168.

Of course the Dow Jones overall began to soar in early 2013. It was at 12,588 in mid-November 2012 and then rose to 14,000 in February 2013 and spiked to 16,000 in November of that year.

Likewise, Raytheon, Lockheed Martin, and Northrop Grumman stocks only continued to rise, but was this only because of the market rise in general? The answer is no, and the reason is U.S. defense spending. Major defense spending cuts began in 2010, and the defense budget was cut 21 percent from 2010 to 2015. The majority of the cuts came independently of the winding down of the Iraq and Afghanistan wars.

It's also important to keep in mind that although U.S. defense spending is down since 2012, it is still significantly higher than it was before September 11, 2001. That day's unconventional attacks on New York and Washington were the seminal events in propelling U.S. defense spending to what would have been considered astronomical levels prior to that fateful day. Defense spending more than doubled from 2001 to 2008.

What alert Newsvestors would have noticed since the Budget Control Act of 2011—which ushered in sequestration, or automatic defense cuts—was that although the U.S. government had decided that increased military spending wasn't necessary in the post–Iraq War world, events worldwide—many events—continued to indicate that war had hardly become a thing of the past. As summarized by the Hanson piece in the *Weekly Standard,* it may well have been America's new inclination to stand down militarily that promoted more conflict around the world—and thus a renewed need for weapons systems and other arms by other countries.

It was critical during this time for Newsvestors to realize that even as the American government cut defense spending, other countries were having to spend more to make up for it. And who provides the lion's share of the arms used by many foreign militaries? U.S. companies.

AMERICA ARMS THE WORLD

Consider this July 2014 story from the *Financial Post* of Britain:

> Today's [geopolitical landscape] . . . is full of the most acute tribal tensions and intense nationalization not seen since the peak of the Cold War era three decades ago. . . . We have China-Japan tensions mounting. . . . Of course, there is

> also Vladimir Putin's complicated game playing out in Ukraine and possibly all of NATO in the process; Iraq's deadly Shia-Sunni sectarian war; Pakistan is at war; Afghanistan is succumbing to Taliban assaults; Syria is a bastion of instability; and North Korea continues to poke its southern neighbor in the eye with repeated projectiles. . . . Even the European Union is riddled with internal conflict.

Eight months earlier, in December 2013, the *Boston Globe* observed, "The Obama administration is making an aggressive push to help U.S. weapons manufacturers sell more arms overseas, including lobbying foreign leaders to purchase warships, aircraft, and missiles, and relaxing some controls on the transfer of military components, according to administration and industry officials."

Indeed, our three sample companies—Lockheed Martin (LMT), Northrop Grumman (NOC), and Raytheon (RTN)—in 2013 were already winning more foreign military contracts before the Obama administration's announced push for more foreign sales for military contractors. The following are just a few examples:

+ "U.S. Deal with Saudis Means $253 Million for Lockheed." The article by Zacks Equity Research reported, "Half of the company's top line is expected to come from foreign governments over the next five years."
+ In May 2013, a Google news search for "Raytheon foreign contracts" turned up this headline from the news outlet Al Arabiya: "Kerry to Help Seal $2.1 Billion Raytheon Defense Deal with Oman."
+ In June 2013, the Motley Fool featured the headline "Northrop Wins $115 Million in Foreign Military Sales Contracts."

The best example of the impact of the shift in both foreign policy and defense-related matters that resulted from the Obama administration can be found in a March 2015 story by *The National,* which is one of the leading online English-speaking news sites concerning the Middle East. The headline said it all: "Saudi Arabia Becomes Biggest Defense Equipment Importer with $9.8 Billion to Be Spent This Year." The article noted that the Saudis leap to becoming the world's biggest importer of defense equipment occurred in great part due to the events following the Arab Spring and the rise of ISIS. The article also observed that "instability in Libya, Yemen, Syria, and Iraq" all played a role in this acceleration in military spending. Top experts expressed the view that those concerns, coupled with a long-standing threat from Iraq, produced "an immediate military threat emerging in the Saudi periphery."

Newsvestors who caught the wave of the post–Arab Spring lift in defense stock prices could likely feel sure of continued strength in their investment. Analysts generally stated that the rapid growth in arms purchases by the Saudis and other nations in the Middle East from U.S.-based companies showed no evidence of slowing down in 2015.

With the Middle East having become the world's fastest growing defense market, U.S. defense-related companies were the chief beneficiaries. The United Arab Emirates and Saudi Arabia alone imported more arms from the United States in 2014 than did all of Western Europe combined. From the *Guardian* in March 2015, "The biggest beneficiary of the strong Middle Eastern market remains the US, with $8.4bn worth of Middle Eastern exports in 2014, compared to $6bn in 2013."

Those are the generalities. But what about the specifics. A grand total is an impressive number, but digging deeper allows for examples of targeted investments, past and present.

PATRIOT MISSILES

A winning strategy for Newsvestors is often to follow the news not just for the names of manufacturers but for their products. Not Raytheon, for example, but the Patriot missiles they manufacture.

Patriots are antiaircraft and antiballistic missiles. They have been manufactured since the early 1980s, but they didn't become well known to the media and the general public until Operation Desert Storm in early 1991. Until then, Patriots were unproven.

During the 1991 war there were forty attempted intercepts of incoming Iraqi missiles. How many of those Patriot intercepts successfully hit their targets is still a matter of dispute. But to Newsvestors, what's important is that what was once considered a *Star Wars* fantasy was, during this short war, proven to be a reality—and a sign of things to come in warfare.

On January 19, 1991, just two days after ground hostilities commenced, a *New York Times* article announced, "Incoming Iraqi Missile Destroyed over

Saudi Base." The report declared, "In its maiden flight of destruction, the American-made Patriot missile won the gratitude of thousands of soldiers and civilians this morning as it blew an Iraqi Scud missile out of the sky over one of Saudi Arabia's largest air bases."

A new technology—and a new investment opportunity—was born for the alert Newsvestor. On the day the ground war started, Raytheon stock sold at $69 per share. On February 28, the last day of the conflict, it sold at $76. And the price climbed to $87 on August 20.

Note also that not even a disastrous failed launch of a Patriot deterred investors. On February 26 of that year, a *New York Times* headline read "Scud Missile Hits U.S. Barracks, Killing 27." The lead explained, "An American Patriot Missile battery in Dhahran, Saudi Arabia, failed to track and intercept an incoming Iraqi Scud missile. The Scud struck an American Army barracks, killing 28 soldiers and injuring around 100 other people." Raytheon stocks continued their price climb anyway. The world—and investors—were convinced that Patriot missiles were here to stay.

By Operation Desert Shield, the beginning of the Second Iraq War in early 2003, Patriot missiles were no longer a novelty to the military, the public, or investors. Patriots had a good record of successfully shooting down enemy missiles, as noted in this April 1 article from the BBC online: "Patriot missile unit stays on target." The report said, "The efficiency of the Patriot batteries—particularly in bringing down Iraqi missiles heading for Kuwait—has been one of the success stories of the U.S.-led war so far."

Since 1991, Raytheon stocks performed so well that the stock split, creating more shares at a lower face value. Consequently, Raytheon at the outset of the war sold at $28 per share. By June 30, four months after the successful initial invasion, it sold at $32. One year later each was worth $35. The stock then split again, providing investors with two shares for one in March 1992.

Eleven years later, in 2014, Raytheon shares received another dramatic boost when the Israeli military launched Operation Protective Edge. Israeli Patriot batteries destroyed two incoming Hamas missiles. Then on July 14, a Patriot missile for the first time intercepted a manned enemy aircraft.

Sure enough, Raytheon share prices jumped from $93 on July 11 to $97 on July 22. On February 11, 2015, they were worth $107. At least fourteen nations now have Patriot missile batteries.

DRONES

Less than a generation ago, it would have seemed miraculously futuristic to imagine a device you could hold in your hand in the middle of nowhere and chat with the family back home. Today that device is as familiar and everyday as the shirt on your back—it's called a cell phone.

A similar market transition is about to happen with drones. Most Americans think of drones as exotic science-fiction contraptions. Upon top-secret orders from the president, drones assassinate terrorists and then vanish. Right?

That's about to change in a big way. The Federal Aviation Administration in February 2015 proposed a detailed set of federal regulations for the use of commercial drones in U.S. airspace. The new rules are set for operations to begin in 2017. Over the coming years, drones are going to become commonplace, as everyone from law enforcement to mom-and-pop stores may be using them. (Yes, they will become that cheap; drone-building kits can be had today for as little as a few hundred dollars.)

Alert Newsvestors would have seen an opportunity upon reading headlines such as "Jobs for Drones Are Set to Take Off." The article reported, "'Some people think that the commercial market for unmanned aircraft systems can be much bigger than the military market,' said Steven Gitlin, vice president of marketing and communications of AeroVironment, a drone manufacturer."

A Google alert for "drones" would have yielded a news report at the Investor Ideas website: "Drone Stocks Added to Tech Stock Directory." Among the ten companies listed as investments because of their manufacturing of drones were Lockheed Martin and Northrop Grumman as well as Boeing, Facebook, and Google. Familiar names to be sure.

Also in February 2015 came news that the Pentagon had opened the legal road for American companies to sell military drones overseas. According to Investors.com, "As the multibillion-dollar market for military and commercial drones gains traction, Lockheed Martin and Raytheon are just two firms that could benefit from the State Department's newly announced policy on expanding drone exports to allies."

As early as February 2013 it was reported that drones were being used by at least fifty countries. Vigilant Newsvestors would have noted this headline from *Voice of America*: "China Drone Threat Highlights Global Arms Race."

Just two days later, ABC News published an article with the headline "Domestic Drones Inch Closer to the Sky Near You," which went on to explain how drones would begin to be used for everyday tasks in the civilian world.

Raytheon stocks enjoyed a meteoric spike in prices over the next two years. Northrop Grumman enjoyed similar stock price growth into early 2015.

But the drone action was not limited to big-name companies. Sometimes monitoring news organizations that are critical of U.S. allies can be just as effective as relying on U.S. or Western-based news organizations.

One such publication routinely savages the Israeli government and its actions. But in doing so, it often provides hugely helpful hints to investors in the United States.

WE DON'T HAVE ALL THE FUN

Recall the earlier discussion of Elbit Systems Ltd.(ESLT), a thinly-traded company followed by only a few analysts. A very unfriendly article about the company from a pro-Palestinian news organization offered this observation:

> US-traded shares of Elbit have climbed 6.1 percent since 8 July, when Israel began its latest offensive against the Gaza Strip. . . .
>
> Elbit's Hermes drone is one of the most widely used by the Israeli army, particularly in the Gaza Strip, where the Hermes 450, outfitted to carry two medium range missiles, has been heavily deployed against civilians in Gaza.
>
> Marketed as "combat-proven" on the company's website, the Hermes 450 drone boasts "300,000 operational flight hours and a class-leading safety and reliability record," a bold declaration for a product that, according to Human Rights Watch, was used by the Israeli army to deliberately target civilians in Gaza during Israel's 2008–2009 onslaught, which killed 1,400 Palestinians, including at least 400 children.
>
> The Hermes drone was also used to kill civilians in Israel's war on Lebanon in 2006, including Red Cross workers, ambulance drivers and dozens of people fleeing their homes

in a desperate and futile search for safety from Israeli bombardment.

Apparently impressed by the aircraft's capacity for bloodshed, the Brazilian government purchased them to help crush the massive protests that erupted across Brazil against the recent World Cup.

In a deal worth $280 million, the Swiss government last month purchased the Hermes 900, a surveillance version of the more deadly Hermes 450.

Elbit is also involved in a $1.6 billion joint venture with Thales, a French weapons company, to develop a drone similar to the Hermes 450 for the UK defense ministry.

Wow. That description might lead a casual investor to move on. But Newsvestors would have learned of Elbit if they were at all interested in potential investment opportunities arising out of the prolonged negotiations for a nuclear deal between the Obama administration and Iran.

As far back as the early 2000s, websites such as one simply called Boycott Israel carried a long description of Elbit that included this again unflattering introduction:

> Elbit Systems is one of Israel's largest security and defense firms, specializing in military electronics, surveillance systems, UAVs (unmanned aerial vehicles, or drones) and homeland security systems. It supplies the Occupation military, navy and air force with a variety of equipment, and has profited greatly from Israel's numerous attacks and assaults on the Palestinian and Lebanese people.

The argument from all sides of the unending conflict in that region notwithstanding, Elbit should have caught Newsvestors' eyes. And as an agreement over Iran's future nuclear programs appeared increasingly likely, Newsvestors could have positioned themselves for a meteoric gain.

As mentioned, on January 2, 2015, Elbit Systems closed on the NASDQ in the $60 range. But as Obama's push for an Iranian agreement gained increased news exposure on a daily basis and unrest in the region continued, the stock shot up to $83 by April. The reelection of Benjamin Netanyahu helped the stock along, but in reality it was moving rapidly higher even as polls suggested a potential defeat for Israel's prime minister.

While Newsvesting is primarily finding long-term investments based on good opportunities to enter and see growth, the example of Elbit, given the fact that it is thinly traded and tied to the fortunes or concerns of Israel, offered Newsvestors more of a short-term play. A $15-to-$22 per-share profit in four months would be nothing to sneeze at, and something to consider pocketing, even if the taxes on that short-term profit would be a bit higher.

With drones in general, it's important for Newsvestors to realize that there isn't one geopolitical event that sharply increased the value of the stocks of drone manufacturers overnight. Instead, this has been a gradually unfolding phenomenon. The news coverage has been there, steady if sporadically, for years. It's been up to alert Newsvestors to connect the dots.

SWING TRADING

The Elbit saga requires us to examine Newsvestors who were or are swing traders, namely, those who buy and sell stock based on short-term fluctuations in the stock market as a whole. The following timeline of Dow readings before, during, and after the First Iraq War can be instructive. It's an example of how a major global news story can clearly and undeniably affect the stock market. So let's return where we started, in 1990, and assume Newsvestors of that day could have easily accessed news and information from across the globe. (This was years later before the World Wide Web would allow for such, but the events and results are highly instructive.)

August 2, 1990: The BBC reported, "More than 100,000 Iraqi soldiers backed up by 700 tanks invaded the Gulf state of Kuwait in the early hours of this morning. Iraqi forces have established a provisional government and their leader Saddam Hussein has threatened to turn Kuwait city into a 'graveyard' if any other country dares to challenge the 'take-over by force.' In response to the news of the invasion the price of oil rose dramatically and stock markets around the world have fallen."

One day later, the Dow Jones dropped 90 points to 2809.

August 5, 1990: President George H. W. Bush referred to the Iraqi invasion as "naked aggression" that will not stand. He signed executive orders freezing both Iraqi and Kuwaiti assets in the United States to deny Hussein access to the funds. And he told the media that he's already working through the State Department to build a united international front. Bush said he wasn't ruling any options in, but he wasn't ruling any out either.

As war clouds gathered, the next day the Dow fell more than 90 points to 2716.

August 7, 1990: Fearing Saudi Arabia's oil fields were next on Iraq's hit list, President Bush sent Secretary of Defense Dick Cheney to the Middle East and then said, "The Saudi government requested our help. And I responded to that request by ordering U.S. forces to deploy to the Kingdom of Saudi Arabia." He also said the sovereign independence of Saudi Arabia was of vital interest to the United States, and that the United States would work with Saudi and other forces to deter further Iraqi aggression. "The multi-national force will enhance the capability of the Saudi forces to defend the Kingdom." The first U.S. forces to arrive were F-15 fighters from Langley Air Force Base in Virginia. The United States then deployed two carrier groups and two battleship groups to the Persian Gulf as well as numerous Air Force units.

Three days later, after falling a bit more, the Dow stabilized at 2716.

August 22, 1990: Hussein didn't blink. So President Bush authorized the first call-up of U.S. military reservists for service in Operation Desert Shield. The first active-duty tours were for 90 days but would extended to 180 days in November 1990.

The Dow took a nosedive to 2560. But it hadn't reached its nadir yet.

October 11, 1990: Economic sanctions had not done the trick. Still no Iraqi capitulation. And the Dow dropped to 2365, down 444 points since the invasion of Kuwait.

November 8, 1990: Realizing military might was probably the only language the Iraqis would understand, Bush beefed up the military in Saudi Arabia and dropped a few hints that coalition forces might attack the Iraqi army.

Investors liked the news, and the Dow rose to 2443.

November 29, 1990: The normally placid U.N. Security Council entered the game and demanded Hussein withdraw his troops "or else." (Resolution 678 gave Iraq until January 15, 1991, to withdraw entirely from Kuwait and restore its national sovereignty.)

More good news for investors. The Dow went up to 2518.

January 17, 1991: Operation Desert Storm began when British, American, Kuwait, French, and Saudi aircraft bombed military and strategic targets in Iraq, including an oil refinery and the Baghdad airport.

A good start rallied the Dow 115 points.

But Saddam was not about to give up without a fight. The Iraqis fought back, and the Dow stalled at 2603.

February 22, 1991: A month of airstrikes continued to pound Iraq unabated, and the market was resurgent. Dow closed at 2889. And the next day, the U.S.-led ground war began.

February 28, 1991: It was all over six days later; Hussein effectively surrendered and the war was quickly over. The market stayed remarkably stable during the weeklong hostilities, finishing at 2882.

March 5, 1991: The shouting commenced in earnest. Military victory was assured, and the Dow rallied to 2972. It later peaked at 2999 in July. That's a gain of almost 10 percent in less than a year. (What makes this doubly remarkable was the fact that oil prices spiked during this time, causing a brief recession.)

While even the most astute Newsvestor might not have been able to pinpoint the exact day to execute trades, knowledge of military buildups and increased rhetoric would have narrowed down the possibilities dramatically. Once President Bush put together the coalition, there was little doubt action would be forthcoming sooner rather than later.

ABOUT THOSE IRANIAN NUKES

A short-term deal can also have long-term effects. Throughout 2014 and well into 2015, the possibility of Iran's enriching enough uranium to build nuclear weapons had, if possible, heated up the Middle East tinderbox even more than usual. Combined with the land grab by ISIS terrorists, several countries in the region, most notably Jordan, Saudi Arabia, and, of course, Israel, sought to strengthen their defense capabilities as much as possible.

Russia entered the mix in April 2015 by ending a 2010 arms embargo against Iran and agreeing to sell the country advanced S-300 surface-to-air missiles. Israel has treated S-300s as a red line, knowing that if Iran has them, they effectively negate Israel's ability to launch an airstrike. In an NBC report, Ben Goodlad, principal weapons analyst for HIS Aerospace, Defense and Security, said, "The sale of S-300 systems to Iran does not pose a direct threat to Israel; however, it would make any potential future airstrikes by the Israeli Air Force more challenging."

As for my Newsvesting in defense stocks, my picks were long-term in nature, including my purchases of Elbit (ESLT). It would be fair to say that most of the companies I bought, including Lockheed Martin (LMT) and Northrop Grumman (NOC), began to move up or down with the market as a whole by the summer of 2015.

But each of my picks paid reasonably strong dividends (Elbit not so much, but fantastic growth!), which served as an additional incentive to hold these picks as part of my portfolio. If the market endured a correction at some point in the future, these stocks would likely drop as well. But if that were to occur down the road, it would present a great opportunity to dollar-cost average my overall price per share and wait for the next set of international incidents that would likely propel these companies to even higher ground.

In toto, the hot spots get hotter and the warm spots continue to heat up. Newsvestors are aware of not only the rhetoric but the smaller actions being taken before the bigger ones become front-page headlines. If Iran via Russia ups the ante, what must possible future targets do to counter such measures? And none of this even mentions China and its increasing militant attitude.

Smart Newsvestors, like smart countries, know the best defense is a good offense.

ISSUE 5 Obama Administration Reaction to Arab Spring

INITIAL EVIDENCE

September 2011, *Wall Street Journal*: "Geriatric U.S. Arsenal Needs Expensive Facelift."

December 2013, *Boston Globe*: "Obama administration making aggressive push to help U.S. weapons manufacturers sell more arms overseas."

EXTENDED EVIDENCE

May 2013, Al Arabiya: "Kerry to help seal $2.1 billion Raytheon defense deal with Oman."

June 2013, Motley Fool: "Northrop Wins $115 Million in Foreign Contracts."

February 2013, Voice of America: "China Drone Threat Highlights Global Arms Race."

July 2014, Financial Post of Britain: "Today's geopolitical landscape is full of the most acute tribal tensions . . . and nationalization . . . since peak of Cold War."

February 2015, "Lockheed Martin and Raytheon are just two of the firms that could benefit from . . . newly announced policy on expanding drone exports."

ISSUE 6 Obama Push for Nuclear Treaty with Iran

INITIAL EVIDENCE

News reports on Obama administration's intent to reach an agreement on "nuclear weapons in Iran" increase in intensity and volume as 2014 ends and 2015 begins.

EXTENDED EVIDENCE

March 3, 2015, Israeli Prime Minister Benjamin Netanyahu speaks to Joint Session of Congress to warn of dangers of a U.S. backed nuclear agreement with Iran.

ISSUE 5 Obama Administration Reaction to Arab Spring

ANALYSIS

U.S. military equipment old and spending down, but exports to nations dealing with fallout from Arab Spring are increasing with U.S. assistance. Consider large-cap defense companies that provide needed weapons, defense systems, cyber-defense, and drones to other nations. Also keep in mind longer-term likelihood that U.S. will have to increase defense spending post-Obama administration much like U.S. increased spending post-Carter administration.

CONCLUSION/ACTION

Purchase Northrop Grumman (NOC) in February 2015 and June 2015 at averaged price of $166 a share. Hold NOC as it rises toward $173 on report second quarter earnings in 2015. Purchase Lockheed Martin (LMT) three times. First in October 2014 at $190 a share. Then in February 2015 at $205.90 a share. Then in June 2015 at 187.60 a share. Hold as LMT reaches $208 a share in July. Purchase Raytheon (RTN) twice in 2015 at average cost of $104 a share. Hold as RTN rises to $109 in July of 2015.

RESULT

Hold all with gains in all three and enjoy strong dividend/yield as well.

ISSUE 6 Obama Push for Nuclear Treaty with Iran

ANALYSIS

Begin process of researching top defense firms that supply Israel with drones, antiballistic systems, and other defense equipment and technology. Pro-Palestinian news source names Elbit Systems (ESLT) as major source of drones to Israel, including the Hermes system. Research back to 2000 shows anti-Israeli sites naming Elbit as major manufacturer of Israeli defense systems. Further research shows Elbit sales strong elsewhere in the world.

CONCLUSION/ACTION

Elbit Systems continues its rise as Iran talks proceed. Purchase ESLT with understanding that strength of company is strong orders for sales to other countries, not just Isreal.

RESULT

Purchase ELST at various prices in the $70 range in March and June 2015. Hold ESLT as it bounces between $72 low in May 2015 to high of around $83 in July. Sold at that time with decision to invest again upon anticipated dip or correction in market later in 2015.

CHAPTER **8**

Déjà Vu
with Smokes and Cokes

To repeat a crucial concept, one of the fundamental principles of Newsvesting is to seek direct correlations between news events—headlines—and the price of a particular stock or stocks. For example, the Affordable Care Act becomes law, and the stocks of private healthcare providers increase in value; a war breaks out, and the prices of defense stocks go up.

Alas, it's not always that simple. Sometimes a headline or a published report can have an effect that might be difficult to isolate as the one and only factor affecting stock prices. The solution is to double down on your vigilance regarding the stock in question and the news that may or may not be influencing its price.

Cigarette manufacturers provide an instructive example. Altria, formerly known as Philip Morris, for example, is a Virginia-based company and one of the largest makers of tobacco products in the world. Among its twenty-three brands of cigarettes are Marlboro, Benson & Hedges, and Virginia Slims. In a seven-year period ending in 2004, Altria spent more than $100 million on lobbying in Washington. That's the second-most spending of any lobbying interest for that period.

Lawsuits against tobacco manufacturers have become commonplace. How does the news—good or bad, from Altria's perspective—affect the company's stock value?

The short answer to that very broad question is that these suits often affect share prices in a significant way.

At the same time, lawsuits against tobacco companies are sometimes considered by the companies and most of its shareholders as merely the price of doing business. While cigarette makers sometimes have to pony up goodly amounts of cash as part of lawsuit settlements, the suits apparently don't greatly reduce the consumption of cigarettes—or the long-term profits for shareholders. The short- and intermediate-term can, of course, be a different story.

Take the Tobacco Master Settlement Agreement of 1998. Altria, then still known as Philip Morris, was one of four major cigarette makers targeted in a suit brought by the attorneys general of forty-six states. (The other three were R. J. Reynolds, Brown & Williamson, and Lorillard.) The settlement of the suit in November 1998 provided compensation to these states for the recovery of money to reimburse the expense of tobacco-related healthcare costs. The settlement also exempted Altria and the other three companies from tort liability regarding smokers of their cigarettes. The companies agreed to pay in excess of $200 billion to the forty-six states over twenty-five years. Two hundred billion! Probably the biggest winners were the plaintiff attorneys, as the following *New York Times* headline pointed out: "The Spoils of Tobacco Wars; Big Settlement Puts Many Lawyers in the Path of a Windfall."

Logic would dictate that the biggest losers were the tobacco companies. Sure enough, Altria share prices declined gradually over a four-year span—but then they rebounded with a vengeance. Here's a sample with all stocks listed at their historical adjusted price.

+ November 1998 (right after the settlement was announced): $5.30 a share. By November 2002 it was at $4.44 a share.
+ In February 2003, shares traded around $4.62. Philip Morris became Altria, adding more products to its tobacco products. By January 2007 the shares reached $12.77.
+ In April 2008, Philip Morris International was spun off as a subsidiary of Altria. The cigarette part of the business was back in one fold. Today, it is the leading international tobacco company, with seven of the world's top fifteen brands, including Marlboro, the number-one cigarette brand worldwide.
+ Philip Morris International's April 2015 price was around $85 per share. Altria was in the $50 range.

Not too shabby for an industry that had been counted down and out years earlier. And the same pattern held true for the other big tobacco companies as well.

If you were a shareholder in R. J. Reynolds (RAI) stock in July 2014, you doubtless would have been alarmed by this headline in *Time* online: "$23.6 Billion Lawsuit Winner to Big Tobacco: Are You Awake Now?"

The article reported:

> [The legal case that paved the way for this settlement] established that the tobacco industry had deceived Americans, by knowingly putting addictive and cancerous products on the market, and paved the way for thousands of individual Florida cases to take on Big Tobacco. On Friday July 18, Cynthia Robinson did, and won her bittersweet victory.

The usual course of events is that huge tobacco settlement amounts like this one are later reduced, as this one was. But there was no guarantee of that in July 2014, and the uncertainty among R. J. Reynolds shareholders reflected that in these share prices immediately following the $23 billion verdict:

+ July 14: $61.26
+ July 18: $56.87
+ August 1: $54.06

But the stocks began to recover their value shortly after that, and rose steadily up to the end of April 2015, when a single share would cost you $73.

And, yes, the lawsuit verdict against R. J. Reynolds also affected, if briefly, the share prices of Altria stocks. Note these prices just before and immediately after the R. J. Reynolds verdict:

+ July 11: $41.97
+ July 17: $40.26
+ August 1: $39.21
+ September 9: $42.26

Overall, big tobacco stocks since their recovery from the 1998 master suit have shown a remarkable resiliency in the face of lawsuits and other setbacks, as indicated in this March 2015 headline from *Seeking Alpha*: "As Altria Keeps Rising, So Does the Temptation to Sell."

This analysis, which was retrieved by a Google news alert, reported:

> Altria is a beloved stock for its long history of providing tremendous returns. According to Altria's investor relations website, Altria's total shareholder return for the five years ending December 31, 2014, was 230 percent. In addition, it is one of the most highly regarded dividend stocks of all time, and for good reason. Altria has increased its dividend 48 times in the last 45 years.

Be that as it may, it's plain that lawsuits do affect stock prices of big tobacco companies, but usually for the short term only. Lawsuits with big price tags, however, aren't the only bad publicity that can affect share prices. Note this headline in February 2015 from the Huffington Post: "Tobacco Giants Battle New Ads Painting Them as Liars."

The article said:

> Bloodied but unbeaten, the tobacco companies have plunged into another courtroom battle in an effort to stave off the humiliation of having to underwrite an ad campaign in which they brand themselves as liars. . . .
>
> The ads would appear in newspapers, on TV, websites and cigarette pack inserts. The ads, called "corrective statements," stem from a civil case the government brought in 1999 under RICO, the Racketeer Influenced and Corrupt Organizations Act.

The result? Altria sells at $53.50 in early February following the story. By early March it had gained an additional $3 per share.

Again, wouldn't logic tell you that with all these beat downs in the courts and public opinion, tobacco would be rendered dead in the water? Hardly. The theme that seems to be emerging is the resiliency of big tobacco stocks. Consider this point by *Seeking Alpha* in March 2015:

> Altria's tremendous returns over the past few years have not been backed up by its fundamentals. The stock is rallying,

which has provided its investors with huge paper gains, but this was due almost entirely to multiple.expansion, and not underlying growth.

In other words, tobacco stocks appear to thrive on the perception that much of the public's apparent addiction to, or at least great fondness for, cigarettes make these stocks invincible. And the comparative strength of these stocks in the face of the headwinds of bad publicity and big lawsuit payouts demonstrates that they appear to be good investments even during periods of economic and stock-market downturns.

In fact, the argument that big tobacco stocks are overvalued seems weaker when it's considered that overvalued stocks are by definition susceptible to so-called corrections. Wouldn't $23 billion in lawsuit damages serve as just such a correction? Yet most of the time it doesn't. As mentioned, apparently these suits are seen by most investors as simply the price of doing business, much like paying taxes.

Moderately good legal news for big tobacco often yields moderately good news for its shareholders. On April 8, 2015, a headline from Reuters announced, "US Appeals Court Deals Setback to Florida Tobacco Plaintiffs." The report said:

> A U.S. appeals court ruling on Wednesday could make it more difficult for smokers suing tobacco companies in Florida to prove claims that cigarettes are dangerous and that tobacco companies were negligent.

In the wake of this, Altria stocks gained about one dollar per share, from $52 to $53 from April 7 to April 10, 2015. R. J. Reynolds shares were $73.71 on April 6 and $74.36 on April 10.

Now let's look at the other end of the dollar-value spectrum for share prices following highly publicized court cases involving big tobacco. On May 22, 2003, the *Wall Street Journal* ran this headline: "Florida Appeals Court Overturns $145 Billion Tobacco Settlement."

The article reported:

> The nation's largest tobacco companies—reeling from a price war with discount brands, slashed credit ratings and

adverse legal rulings—won a significant victory as a Florida
appeals court tossed out a landmark $145 billion judgment
that had threatened to imperil the industry.

This was a major victory for big tobacco and its shareholders, and share prices following the announcement showed it in a big way.

Altria (prices are adjusted prices reflecting historical dividends and splits. Atria was then Philip Morris but under the same stock symbol it has today—MO).

+ April 25: $3.78
+ May 30: $5.03

R. J. Reynolds (historical adjusted prices).

+ April 25: $3.49
+ July 25: $4.70

On the other hand, and interestingly, when the original $145 billion judgment against the tobacco industry was announced in October 1994, share prices for Altria dropped only from $4.70 on October 21 to $4.34 on December 9.

Why does tobacco continue to perform, even in the worst of industry and economic times? Well, as we've pointed out, the product is addictive. Ask anyone who's ever tried to quit. (As a matter of fact, Newsvestors might even want to do some research on the tobacco-quitting industry. There never seems to be a dearth of advertising come-ons for ways to kick the butts.)

Tobacco has also always been part of social gatherings, especially in local watering holes. While family-oriented establishments mostly forbid smoking, if local laws allow, you're not going to find a whole lot of bars that prohibit it.

Tobacco is even viewed as a stress reliever by many, particularly among those in lower socioeconomic areas. Given that they as a group have taken the brunt of economic downturns, especially recently, it's no wonder that tobacco stocks remain good investments. Even reports such as this from Treatobacco fail to dent profits: "The consensus among researchers working in this area is that a 10 percent increase in the price of cigarettes in developed countries will result in a 3 to 5 percent reduction in overall cigarette consumption."

As for my Newsvesting in tobacco, I purchased both Altria and Philip Morris International as part of my portfolio early in 2014 and in 2015. With the dollar rising, conventional wisdom suggested that Altria would flourish, since its sales were only in the United States and not impacted by the strengthening dollar. For Philip Morris, the concept was that a strong dollar would weaken the stock but push the company to higher dividends.

In the end, both did well. When the dollar would start to retreat, Philip Morris International would move higher. And when the dollar strengthened, Altria had the momentum. I sold half of my Altria stock in late May 2015 for a very handsome gain. The other half would balance out the investment in Philip Morris International (one would rise on a strong dollar while the other would likely fall, but both would pay great dividends).

Just as in the political realm, where it can be necessary to put partisanship aside in pursuit of a good financial deal, there may be times when Newsvestors are loathe to consider a sin industry such as tobacco. But lest we forget, we're here to make money. And there's no denying that tobacco company profits are hardly disappearing in a puff of smoke.

THE FIZZ BIZ

An axiom of investing is that no one person can figure out the market. That's because so many factors go into the makeup of the market that for the purpose of comprehension, those factors might as well be infinite.

So how can Newsvestors turn a dime on a particular stock as opposed to just owning an index of stocks and waiting for the years it takes for the stocks to mature?

The answer is to look for opportunities, perhaps infrequent ones, in which a single factor causes a stock's price to change—a single factor that can be identified with relative ease.

That single factor can be as big and broad as the outbreak of war or as modest as the announcement of a company's quarterly earnings. It just has to be a situation in which Newsvestors can correlate an event or events with the price of one or more particular stocks.

Newsvestors would always be wise to keep their eyes peeled for stories related to the strength of the U.S. dollar. I would add gold to this discussion, but frankly so many have extolled the virtue of buying gold while so many others have lampooned these various gold rushes over the years that a decision to start trading it, just like most commodities, is too confusing, complicated, and potentially dangerous for Newsvestors to handle.

But as stories concerning the dollar develop over months and years, it's important to keep a Newsvesting eye on the watch for issues that might spring forth as a result of a weakening or strengthening of the greenback.

Perusing any number of articles that chronicled the rise of the dollar in 2014 and 2015 would produce the same corporate names that are viewed as vulnerable to a strengthening dollar. One of those companies stuck out in 2014, not because of the risk of a strengthening dollar, but because of its ability to persevere while indirectly under attack from various aspects of government, media, and investment experts.

For years there has been a war waged on so-called fast food, junk food, and colas. Starting years ago, cries rang out to remove soda vending machines from high school campuses. That was the result of endless media stories on the supposed dangers of drinking soft drinks such as Coke and Pepsi. And the war against unhealthy food and drinks, most often cloaked as protecting young people, received a major boost when First Lady Michelle Obama made it her cause to bring allegedly healthy (and bland) food to the cafeterias of the nation's schools. (Just ask a kid if you doubt that opinion. He'll be the one brown-bagging lunch every day.) Of course, few missed New York Mayor Michael Bloomberg's attack on the Big Gulp in an effort to ban large servings of sodas in the city.

Missing in all of these battles was the rather common-sense concept of moderation in all things and, certainly, the free choice of consumers or parents of consumers.

As to be expected, in the face of those attacks, the Coca-Cola Company (KO) took its share of attacks and predictions of ruin at the hands of changes in dietary habits along with media and governmental attitudes toward the company's namesake product and its diet version, along with a multitude of other products.

But in looking at shares of the company over the five years since the alleged end of the Great Recession, Coke has performed well, in that it had ups and downs but in a reasonably tight trading range, despite the face of the gloom-and-doom news stories about the company and its future. April 2013 *Money Morning* headlined, "Buy, Sell or Hold? Is Coca-Cola Still the 'Real Thing' for Investors?" That same month, the Motley Fool questioned Coke's largest shareholder's acumen: "Coke Stock. One of Warren Buffett's

Biggest Investments Might Be His Worst." In October 2013, *Seeking Alpha* asked, "Coca-Cola: A Wise or a Foolish Investment?"

The next year it didn't get any better. Jeff Reaves from MarketWatch backed up his "5 great brands that I think are bad investments" headline with this opinion:

> I think Coca-Cola . . . is equally bad for investors. Sure, Coke is great as a caffeinated pick-me-up, but sugary, carbonated beverages are on the decline in the developed world thanks to a focus on fighting childhood obesity and a rise of healthier alternatives. Coca-Cola has tried to hedge its bets with lines like its Odwalla juices and Powerade sports drink, but the flagship soda brands of Coke and Sprite are having trouble fighting upstream. Consider that Coke's stock has added just 8% in the past 24 months, around half that of the S&P 500. The company is certainly entrenched and offers a modest dividend, but investors have plenty of alternatives out there for income and stability, and shouldn't be taken in by the big brand of Coke.

Wintergreen added fuel to the fire in December 2014: "Coca-Cola's Fizzy Math: How Bad Performance, Excessive Pay and Weak Governance Are Harming Shareholders." In its opinion,

> We have been sharply critical of Coca-Cola's poor performance, excessive pay practices and weak governance because they harm all Coca-Cola shareholders. Yet despite criticism from us and from Coca-Cola shareholders, Coca-Cola's management and Board of Directors appear to be doing little to address these problems. Instead of meaningful change, Coke seems to us to be using diversions and obfuscation—what we call fizzy math—in order to continue practices that have failed its shareholders time and again.

Yet shares of Coke opened 2014 at around $40 a share, and by November of that year had bumped up to around $45. And that was with a very nice dividend/yield.

Coca-Cola has been viewed for many years by analysts as more of a dividend play than a huge growth stock. And as Newsvestors, it's smart to seek out strong companies that consistently pay out strong dividends year after year. Even as analysts were at war over the future value of an investment in Coca-Cola, this piece from *Seeking Alpha* appeared in May 2015:

Dividend growth stocks' appeal comes from their steadily rising dividend payments. High quality businesses with strong competitive advantages have a very high probability of raising dividend payments year after year.

Not every business can grow year-in-and-year-out. There are currently only 16 'Dividend Kings' that have grown their dividend payments for 50 or more consecutive years. These businesses have proven over the last 50 years they have strong and durable competitive advantages.

Not every dividend growth stock grows at a rapid pace indefinitely. You don't need them all to grow indefinitely for excellent results. Only a few big winners in a portfolio will provide substantial returns.

Coca-Cola's business model has not changed substantially over the last 25 years. The company still sells non-alcoholic beverages. Coca-Cola already had a well-respected non-carbonated beverage portfolio in 1990. Non-carbonated beverages the company acquired or started by 1990 include: Powerade, BonAqua, Aquarius, Georgia, and Minute Maid.

Over the last 25 years Coca-Cola has continued to expand its carbonated and non-carbonated beverage portfolio globally. The company now has 20 brands with $1 billion or more in annual sales. 8 out of 9 billion dollar brands added since 1990 are non-carbonated. Investors falsely assume Coca-Cola's business model is based solely on sodas. Three new brands joined the billion-dollar club in 2014: Gold Peak Tea, FUZE Tea, and I LOHAS Mineral Water. All 3 are non-carbonated.

Coca-Cola currently has a 3.2% dividend yield. Investors from 1990 have a yield-on-cost of 49% (assumes dividends were reinvested). Coca-Cola stock would pay out your initial investment in dividends in about 2 years' time.

Coca-Cola is still growing. The company has maintained an 11% compound annual growth rate over the last 25 years. Coca-Cola currently trades for a price-to-adjusted-earnings ratio of around 20. The company is trading around its historical price-to-earnings ratio. Coca-Cola is likely at fair value. Investors have the opportunity to pick up this high-quality dividend growth stock at fair prices now. Coca-Cola's combination of a high dividend yield, strong competitive advantage, stability, and growth prospects make it a favorite."

Not everyone, however, thought so highly of Coke. Brian Sozzi, an analyst writing on the site *TheStreet.com,* piled on the bandwagon against Warren Buffett and his devotion to Coke as one of the four largest holdings of his Berkshire Hathaway conglomerate. Sozzi argued:

Coke needs more non-Coke revenue.

Total U.S. carbonated soft-drink sales volume fell 0.9% last year, the tenth-straight year of decline, according to Beverage Digest. Within that category, Coke posted a 1.1% decline in volume, while Pepsi realized a 1.4% decline.

The focus by Coca-Cola execs on smaller package sizes for its regular soda to boost profits, and new low-carb "Life" to placate health conscious consumers, has still left the company overly exposed to waning carbonated soft-drink sales and competitive pricing in the United States. Coke has chosen to invest its vast riches into more ventures in the competitive beverage industry, as opposed to building a complementary snacks business.

In effect, Coke is not acting to widen its economic moat. An economic moat, an important concept often mentioned by Buffett, represents the competitive advantages a business has in place to protect its profits and market share.

But *The Street* founder and the CNBC star Jim Cramer saw things differently. A post carrying his analysis noted:

> Coca-Cola, on the other hand, is intriguing because of its stake in Monster Beverage, and potential homerun stake it also has in Keurig Green Mountain with its new cold drink machine.
>
> [Cramer] also likes the 3 percent yield and possible peak in the dollar versus emerging market currencies, which is good news considering that Coca-Cola is hedged versus the euro and yen.

In other words, Cramer felt Coke could withstand the surge in the dollar's value and liked the company's strong dividend.

And, yes, that strong-dollar issue kept popping up in articles about Coca-Cola.

As noted earlier, Newsvestors in late November of 2014 would have noticed an increasing number of stories focusing on the swift rise of the dollar. Under an October banner of "The Rise of the US Dollar (What it means in your portfolio)," a *Wealth Daily* article said,

> Indications are the dollar will continue to strengthen, as foreign economies continue to reel and their central banks print more money to save them. The USD will not only benefit from foreign central banks knocking their own currencies down, but also from the U.S. central bank when it begins raising interest rates in the not too distant future.
>
> But what does this newfound strength in America's currency mean for our investment portfolios? As the dollar's status shifts, should we be shifting our investments as well?
>
> Before adjusting anything in our portfolios, we need to note why the dollar has been strengthening recently and whether this is a momentary phase or something more permanent.
>
> We continue to believe that the breakout of the U.S. Dollar against other global developed-market currencies is the most important data point for investors to consider in the present environment.

By February and March 2015, the currency market had grown exceptionally volatile, according to economists and currency traders and brokers. Its effect on American companies that export their products overseas was significant.

Newsvestors following the dollar in early 2015 would have seen numerous headlines basically proclaiming "Coca-Cola and Pepsi Face Obstacle as U.S. Dollar Surges." Maine News Online reported, "The biggest problem that Coca-Cola and Pepsi face these days is the increasing US dollar as both companies have a significant percentage of revenue [roughly half] from their overseas markets. . . . Against major currencies, the dollar has increased 17 percent over the last year." If Newsvestors had sought confirmation of the dollar's new strength from a more renowned news source, there were many examples, including this headline from a report published on February 20, 2015, by the Associated Press: "Rising Dollar Takes Toll on US Corporate Profits; More Pain Ahead."

The rise in the dollar's value meant that when beverage bottlers and retailers in foreign countries exchanged their weakening currencies for the dollars it took to buy Coke, they didn't get as much cola in their glasses as they used to. Put another way, the price of Coca-Cola products had gone up overseas, and that had cost Coke sales and profits—and driven down the price of its stock here at home.

Sure enough, Coke's stock on February 20, when the first article above was published, was $41.97 a share. Just three weeks later, it had dropped to $39.91. This was doubly bad news for Coke, because the company's domestic sales continued to be threatened by those nutrition crusaders who have condemned soda drinks as unhealthy.

But there is a secret just as important to Coca-Cola as the famed secret formula that makes up the syrup to create the real thing. That secret is that Coke has for many decades seen revenues and profits soar when the dollar was weak and lost some fizz when the dollar started to rise. Because Coca-Cola has traditionally chosen not to hedge against such currency fluctuations to the degree of many other multinational companies who depend significantly on foreign sales, the company's stock tends to react more substantially to the rise and fall of the dollar.

While that may seem like a bad thing, for those who truly believe in the inherent value of a company, buying during a run up in the strength of the dollar can prove to be a wise long-term investment. And that helps defeat those who will argue that Newsvesting is really advocating short-term trading.

In the end, there were arguments running in both directions as to whether the Coca-Cola Company had the right mix of products or could withstand the increasing health-conscious consumer in the years to come.

But what most admitted was that the company had so many products with such worldwide distribution and such high value that, if one were to break off and sell whole segments of the world of Coca-Cola, the revenue that would be created would be staggering.

The Newsvesting process and a little bit of historical research as to charts of past rises in the dollar and their correlation to drops in the price per share on Coca-Cola confirmed that as the dollar rose in value between October 2004 and October 2005, Coke stock remained relatively flat—gaining a bit as the dollar dropped slightly, only to drop a bit when it rose. In 2007, Coke shares crested as the dollar, in mid-July of that year, dropped quickly. In 2008, as the dollar resurged prior to the late financial meltdown of October 2008, Coca-Cola shares dropped significantly. But as 2008 advanced, so did Coke shares as the dollar declined. And in 2009, as the dollar remained weak, Coke shares rose.

If anything, as Jim Cramer suggested, Coke was better hedged against a strong dollar in 2015 than in earlier years. Still, the obvious inverse correlation existed and was cited by Coke CEO Muhtar Kent in discussing first quarter 2015 results.

For Newsvestors looking for stock in a solid company that paid good dividends, Coca-Cola seemed prime for consideration. But in the balancing out of evidence pro and con, the strengthening of the dollar made Coke a more attractive buy. Why? Because any discount (decreased price per share) on the cost of buying Coke stock during a strengthening dollar would pay off in its inherently proven increase in value when the dollar weakens again (as it always does). While some of its competitors outperformed Coca-Cola in recent times, Coke seemed the solid, steady company with strong dividends and one likely to pay out dividends regardless of monetary policy. Which leads to another aspect of Newsvesting: keeping an open mind.

BLASPHEMOUS BUT PRUDENT: I'LL HAVE A PEPSI TOO

In researching the dollar and the merits of Coke as an investment, the name of its rival, Pepsi, was thrown around a lot, and often in a glowing manner. To many analysts, PepsiCo (PEP) was more diversified with its snacks division and more attractive with strong performances in the market in recent times. Because of PepsiCo's potential to grow its dividend in the future, it makes sense to own shares of both Coca-Cola and PepsiCo while choosing dividend-producing stocks that could see a bounce in the value of their shares when the dollar weakens down the road.

For Newsvestors there was the simple issue of price. Coca-Cola was bouncing around the low to mid-$40 range in 2014 and early 2015 while PepsiCo was at the mid-$80 range, bumping its head at around $100 a share through that same period. In a sense, PepsiCo was a hedge on Coca-Cola, so to speak. But it was twice as expensive. The Newsvesting answer, once convinced that both were strong companies and could bounce on a future weaker dollar, was to have a blend of shares in both companies. The stronger dose would go with Coca-Cola, which had seen its North American revenues increase in the first quarter under a refined strategy by CEO Kent and his team. But mixed in would be a bit of PepsiCo, which seemed the more dynamic of the two companies in the more recent year.

In September 2014, as the avalanche of stories began to appear discussing a recent rise in the strength of the dollar, what was the result of having taken those stories as enough evidence to begin Newsvesting in them both?

The adjusted closing price for Coca-Cola on September 15 following publication of that story was $40.88. From that date through the end of the first quarter of 2015, the stock crossed $44 several days and saw its lowest close at $39 and change. Give or take a few cents, and assuming the purchase of Coca-Cola was long term in nature, the shares would still be owned and selling for right around the same price they were purchased—and still paying out its dependable dividend.

PepsiCo was perhaps more tempting to trade. With an adjusted price at $90 on September 15, PepsiCo would move upward to the mid-$90 dollar range and bump up to near $100 between the purchase date and the release of its first-quarter earnings. After earnings were announced, the stock was still a comfortable $95 a share.

Newsvestors could have purchased PepsiCo in September at around $90, recognized the swift move close to $100, sold off the shares, and repurchased PepsiCo later for around the same price it would settle at after the first-quarter earnings were reported. Certainly, of the two stocks, PepsiCo seemed peppier.

But the real play for Coca-Cola and PepsiCo was the strengthening of the dollar. And while PespiCo has snack divisions, which drove revenue growth, they were also under attack as being unhealthy. That was something PepsiCo spent a great deal of ad and marketing dollars to combat and they fought a two-front war, as opposed to Coca-Cola's primary battle over carbonated beverages.

Zacks, in their analysis of Coke's first-quarter earnings announcement, stated:

> Coca-Cola began 2015 on a strong note beating the Zacks Consensus Estimate for both earnings and revenues in the first quarter despite significant currency headwinds. Excluding the impact of currency, earnings of 48 cents per share increased 15% backed by improved organic revenues and strong margins. Organic revenues increased 8% driven by extra selling days and strong pricing gains.

And Coke had started its strategic initiative program, which *Zacks* described:

> Other than aggressively cutting costs, the plan includes making disciplined brand and growth investments as well as aligning incentive plans. The company is also re-franchising the majority of its company-owned North American bottling territories to create a more efficient system. It closed several transactions in 2014 and plans to complete two-thirds of the re-franchising by 2017-end which should improve margins and drive growth.

But the *Zacks* report added:

> Management expects the macro-economic environment to remain volatile in 2015. While the macro environment is improving in the U.S., management expects to continue to see a sluggish consumer spending environment in other developed nations like Europe and Japan as well as challenges in many key emerging markets like Brazil, Russia and China. Coca-Cola carries a Zacks Rank #3 (Hold).

And in dealing with stocks such as Coca-Cola, *hold* is the operative word. The company's devotion to strong dividends, focused management, more daring investments, such as Monster Drinks, purchased while the dollar was flying high, all suggested that Warren Buffett was right in his continued confidence in Coca-Cola.

As the stock shifted, a dollar-average purchase could be made. Even adding Coca-Cola shares, should they drop over future quarters, would only result in more shares at a lower average price, receiving strong quarterly income off of dividends and with a long history of always coming back.

In my own Newsvesting, I purchased Coca-Cola several times on dips in its price and remained prepared to double down with more purchases as the company's shares potentially dropped over likely interest rates hikes and more strengthening of the dollar. And I followed my gut by holding PepsiCo with its solid dividend as well, with the same long-term strategy in place.

While the rival companies would likely say the two lead brands don't mix, I had a Coke, a smile, and a Pepsi too.

ISSUE 7 Tobacco Companies in News Over Lawsuits, Dollar Strengthening

INITIAL EVIDENCE

2014 news stories abound over likely strengthening of U.S. dollar.

February 2015, *Associated Press*: "The tobacco companies have recently plunged into another courtroom battle in an effort to stave off the humiliation of having to underwrite an ad campaign in which they brand themselves as liars." Altria sells at $53.72.

EXTENDED EVIDENCE

April 8, 2015, Reuters: "U.S. appeals court deals setback to Florida tobacco plaintiffs . . . would make it more difficult for smokers suing tobacco companies in Florida."

Additional research shows past court decision boosting Altria, Philip Morris International, and Reynolds.

ISSUE 7 Tobacco Companies in News Over Lawsuits, Dollar Strengthening

ANALYSIS

Strong dollar helps Altria, and past evidence suggests tobacco stocks rise after legal reverses. Florida is a huge "plaintiff's state," making the decision of the court even more important. Dollar begins to weaken a bit later making Philip Morris stronger (weak dollar PM does well; strong dollar Altria does well).

CONCLUSION/ACTION

Purchase shares of Altria (MO) in 2014. First purchase at $35.31 a share, then later (smaller purchase) in 2014 at $48.38 a share for average of $37.46. Purchase Philip Morris International (PM) twice. First time December 2014, then again mid-January 2015. Both purchases average $82.40.

RESULT

Sell MO in May 2015 with a profit of $12 a share. Purchase again during dip in market in early July. Hold PM as it rises as high as $86 a share and rises as July of 2015 ends. Both stocks provide dividend/yield of over 4%. Prepare to purchase both again on major dip in market expected in late summer 2015.

CHAPTER **9**

Oil—Gooey Mess or Black Gold?

We all know that, much like politicians, news cycles come and go with the wind. A hot topic in Washington or on the cable news channels can soar on for days or weeks, and then suddenly be replaced by another theme that seems to just burst onto the scene, even if it's as seemingly slow-paced as the flow of oil through a pipeline.

It's hard for the most seasoned veteran of political or news or opinion research to spot a trend that might actually impact the financial world and potential investments far ahead of the critical moment. You know, when a certain issue or news theme unexpectedly catches the attention of the media with that "breaking news" or "news alert" heightened sense of importance that we expect many times a day and on every broadcast, whether it's local, national, or international. Oftentimes online stories, because there are so many and they simply keep coming, provide a good first indication of the development of a major news story that might continue to build.

The story behind the not-so-sudden sudden drop in oil prices that started to dominate the news in late 2014 is a great example of how keeping an eye on the preponderance of news stories can provide an opportunity for Newsvestors to hunt down a great investment opportunity, be it short-term or more likely long-term in nature.

As January 2015 dawned, the news was filled with stories of plummeting oil prices and cheaper and cheaper gasoline prices at the pump. And the financial markets felt the shock. They seemed to reel with each new headline about the precipitous drop in the per-barrel price of crude.

By this time, average stockbrokers, or even better retail investment bankers, could tell their clients chapter and verse as to how and why oil production was up while global consumption was declining. But average investors would have to ask, "Where were you with these words of wisdom six months ago?"

It's a question sure to be met with the sound of chirping crickets, economic doublespeak, or a shoulder shrug.

Because many analysts, brokers, and financial advisors back in mid-2014 had been pushing investments not only in the large petrochemical companies, such as ExxonMobil, British Petroleum, and ConocoPhillips, but also in companies that were starting to thrive by fracking, or hydraulic fracturing, which is the process of extracting oil and natural gas from shale rock within the earth. The high price of oil encouraged this more expensive method of production.

But, in reality, the price of crude oil had started to show signs of a potential decline as early as May 2014. Had interested investors simply set up a few Google news alerts on subjects like oil, gasoline, gas prices, and the like, they would likely have been aware that beneath the surface of the business-as-usual oil buzz, there was something significant happening in this industry.

Over the summer months up to the end of the year, vigilant Newsvestors witnessed a classic example of how a news wave builds and builds before crashing, tsunami-like, and roiling financial markets, leaving devastation in its substantial wake. Remember, no less a financial luminary than Warren Buffett subscribes to the practice of being a news and information hawk. He is devoted to reading everything he can to keep up with business and investment trends.

Now, were we talking about investing in a start-up industry or a small stock, it would be more understandable how projections on the future value of a stock or a business could be so inaccurate. But oil? Oil is an industry in which billions of dollars routinely change hands regularly. Finance magnates have highly trained experts to advise them on if, when, and how much to invest. How could such a shift in both supply and demand have happened so quickly? And why did it take until around October 2014 for a slew of online and print articles to suddenly emerge about oil-related industries and, ultimately, the world economy?

The simplest explanation is that future projections of a longstanding industry like the mining of oil are typically based on history. In mid-June 2014, oil was trading at more than $110 a barrel. Many in the mainstream media and even on Wall Street saw no reason to think things were going to change anytime soon.

Note this June 13 *USA Today* article: "Escalating tensions in Iraq spilled over to energy markets for a second day Friday, pushing crude oil prices to ten-month highs and setting the stage for stubbornly high gasoline prices in the U.S. to rise even further."

Investors might easily have taken this news as a prompt to further invest in oil companies and other businesses whose fortunes are tied to oil drilling and production. But just a week later, oil prices started a decline that would soon become precipitous.

Had our sample Newsvestors set up a series of news alerts, however, the chances are they would have come across a June 9 *Forbes* article titled "9 Reasons Why Oil Prices May Be Headed for a Bust." (Notice the headline said *bust* and not just *decline*.)

Among the reasons for this projected slump in oil prices were a tightening money supply, increased supply from shale oil, and a declining global demand, according to *Forbes*.

The key to the *Forbes* analysis was that it went against the grain of what was generally being said in the media and among financial advisors about oil prices. It didn't rely on repeating past trends, but rather focused on examining new and emerging developments.

For the especially watchful, there were even earlier hints of falling oil prices. On January 2, 2014, *Time* wrote, "Analysts expect gas prices to decrease or remain mostly flat not only in 2014, but for years to come."

On March 29, 2014, the following analysis appeared in *Barron's*: "The long-term outlook for global oil prices is lower, perhaps much lower. . . . Citigroup's head of global commodity research . . . believes the combination of flattening consumption and rising production should mean that 'the $90-a-barrel floor on the world oil price over the past few years will become a $90 ceiling.'"

The Street on May 13, 2014 gave "Three Reasons Oil Prices Will Fall." (The three reasons were [1] OPEC oil production could start to rise, [2] the natural gas market was slowly cooling down, and [3] high imports and production.)

And on June 4 the trade publication Oilprice.com wrote, "Oil demand has been falling across the developed nations and is still weak coming out of the global financial crisis. Those developments point toward a glut [of oil production]."

To Newsvestors carefully tracking the news, the above examples collectively charted a different course for oil prices than was most widely believed at the time. Several different sources—from daily newspapers to oil industry trade journals—all reached similar conclusions, and they did so over a period of months leading up to the oil price decline that lay ahead in the second half of 2014. (Crude oil went for about $110 a barrel in April and May, peaked at about $115 in June, and then started dropping, first to $108 in July and then $98 in September, $80 in November, and $45 in January.)

A growing trend of online, print, and broadcast stories about an issue, such as the steep decline in oil prices in 2014, usually becomes a four-alarm news fire when it becomes front-page news in a major financial paper.

In this particular case that moment came on October 15, 2014, in a front-page, above-the-fold headline in the *Wall Street Journal*: "Global Oil Glut Sends Prices Plunging." A good example of how such a headline impacts an investment can be found by tracing ConocoPhillips' performance both prior to and after the *WSJ* story.

As an historical note, ConocoPhillips (symbol: COP) is today "the world's largest independent exploration and production company, based on proved reserves and production of liquids and natural gas," according to the company website. ConocoPhillips can trace its beginnings to 1875, when Isaac Elder Blake began importing kerosene in bulk by railroad cars from eastern refineries to Ogden, Utah, where people were using candles and whale oil to light their homes. The Phillips brothers—Frank and L. E.—first struck oil seven miles north of Bartlesville, Oklahoma, in 1905. Various mergers and divestments have dotted the company's historical landscape to the present. Today, ConocoPhillips employs over sixteen thousand people in thirty countries.

In July 2014, ConocoPhillips stock was trading in the mid-$80 dollar range. Clearly investors failed to recognize the growing drumbeat of news concerning increasing supplies of crude oil and potential declines in future demand. By early September 2014, the market had started to respond, with ConocoPhillips shares trading in the upper $70 range.

Before big news stories suddenly become bold headline news, reporters have to start asking questions. As those questions are asked, more and more parties who have a vested interest in tracking the particular subject become aware that the story is coming.

By October 13, ConocoPhillips was trading at around $68 per share. On the morning when the *WSJ* story ran, the stock opened at $63.79 and closed that day at $66.20. Had one been involved in true day trading, a practice that would certainly not meet Warren Buffett's philosophy of investing, nor most experts these days, it would be fair to guess that a $2-a-share profit could have been made fairly easily.

The problem with such an approach, except in very rare instances (see above the treatment of Ebola and the airlines), is that such a substantial drop in price per share along with such instability and confusion over the circumstances related to that drop create what is known to the investment community as the "falling knife." With circumstances so hazy and the price dropping so substantially, that falling knife could cut someone pretty badly if they tried to catch it.

CATCHING A FALLING KNIFE
OR PROFITING FROM A BOUNCING BALL

Warren Buffett may well have flinched at the idea of ever purchasing another share of ConocoPhillips. In 2008, when it appeared the world was on the verge of a major energy crisis, he invested billions of dollars into ConocoPhillips. He did so, as he stated later in a letter to shareholders, when oil and gas prices were at nearly an all-time high. In the case of ConocoPhillips, that would likely be a price near $95 a share. And the company changed a great deal between the time Buffett purchased more than $7 billion worth of ConocoPhillips stock and 2014 when he had reduced his holdings substantially. The company sold off Phillips 66 in 2012 and became the world's largest independent exploration and production company.

That transformation probably didn't improve Buffett's purchase of ConocoPhillips, which he termed a "major mistake" by the end of 2008.

But that begs the question: if an investor who is as savvy as Mr. Buffett can make the wrong decision about a company, with his philosophy of usually investing and holding that investment for a very long time, could that same mistake be made in not picking up on another key aspect of his philosophy, which is to look at downturns in the market as buying opportunities? And more important, must an investor hold a stock forever?

Using ConocoPhillips as an example, what happened if an individual purchased ConocoPhillips at its low on the date of the *WSJ* article or even held out longer, until the stock reached a level close to that price, such as was the case of its closing price on December 11, 2014? Had investors done so with a vow to see the stock through from the date of purchase until the end of the year (ConocoPhillips closed on December 31, 2014, at a price of $69.06), and then sell on that date, they would have pocketed a short-term capital gain of over $5 a share.

(Yes, it would have been taxed at ordinary income rates, but it would be nice income to have.)

Even as ConocoPhillips was under pressure from the markets and was slowly being unloaded by Buffett, most analysts had a strong buy, buy, or hold with regard to the stock. That was partly due to its strong dividend/yield.

Oil companies weren't the only ones in play at this time. It's also important to examine the performance of stocks that are related to and affected by oil prices. Consider the stock prices of four companies to see if and how they correlate over the period of several months just mentioned (prices are rounded off to the nearest dollar).

As mentioned, ConocoPhillips is a large petrochemical company that shed its refinery portion (Phillips 66) in 2012. Its stock dropped from $71 per share in November 2014 to $61 in January 2015.

Halliburton is widely renowned for its manufacturing of deep-well drilling equipment and related infrastructure support. Its stock plummeted from $55 in November 2014 to $38 in January 2015.

Emerge Energy Services supplies the fracking or shale oil industry. Recall that this industry during this period was locked in a price war with traditional drillers, especially Saudi Arabia, which some argue purposely oversupplied the world oil market to try to significantly harm the largely American fracking industry. Sure enough, Emerge stock fell from $83 in November to $48 in January.

Tesla manufactures electric cars. As gasoline prices tumble, it might be safe to assume that the market for electric and other alternative energy vehicles might suffer. (It did.) Tesla's stock dipped from $258 in November to $191 in January.

The auto-buying market also was affected. For example, General Motors reported that December 2014 sales improved by 19 percent over December

2013, the biggest jump in seven years. SUV sales were up for several manufacturers. Since most newly purchased vehicles have a service life of at least
seven years, buying gas guzzlers based on what may be a short-term reduction in gasoline prices might be an impulsive choice for consumers.

Similarly, in January 2015, most speculation and analysis centered on
why and how much oil prices would drop. Just as the investment herd stam-
peded to investments in oil and oil-related industries when prices were about
to drop in June, six months later the herd was again charging in unison, but
this time acting as if the trend of falling oil prices would seemingly never
end. So wise Newsvestors might have started to look at news alerts that
hinted at new and future developments that might *increase* the price of oil.

One came as early as December 8, 2014, from the investment newsletter
Seeking Alpha, in a piece titled "Crude Oil: A Bounce Is on the Horizon." The
main reason cited for a prospective price rebound was increasing demand
from an improving U.S. economy.

Then a media bombshell came on January 20 in *USA Today,* which in-
terviewed a former CEO of Shell Oil. In direct contradiction to the prevailing
wisdom, John Hofmeister predicted that gasoline eventually could top $5
per gallon. He pointed to ever-growing worldwide demand as the reason.
"The next round of high prices," he said, "is likely to start later [in 2015], as
crude rebounds to the $80s and $90s, perhaps pushing to the $100 level by
late in the year or early next."

Oil prices bumped up modestly after the *USA Today* article appeared.
This illustrates a key point to any media-based approach to investing: inter-
mediate- or long-term investments in oil and oil-related industries depend
on a wide assortment of market conditions, but short-term investments can
depend partly or even wholly on the *perception* of market conditions in the
major media. The two aren't necessarily always the same.

It's critical here to consider how and why oil prices fell so fast. By November
2014, prices were already falling for natural reasons—production was soaring
in the United States and Canada, and weakening economies in Europe and Asia
were curbing demand.

Then the Organization of Petroleum Exporting Countries (OPEC) met on
November 27. OPEC does not dominate the world oil supply as it once did,
but it still accounts for about 40 percent of the global supply. And those who
thought OPEC's ability to throw its weight around was a thing of the past were
in for a surprise when Saudi Arabia, the kingpin of OPEC, announced it had

no intention of cutting production in order to prop up falling oil prices. Those prices immediately began a steeper plummet to south of $50 a barrel. Saudi Arabia was willing to subsist on its substantial currency reserves in order to force the American shale fracking industry to cut production, because shale drilling is more expensive than traditional deep-well drilling.

What's key for Newsvestors to note is that the precipitous drop in oil prices was not solely the product of natural market conditions, that is, the collective actions of many thousands of investors and oil-business executives to drill or not to drill. Instead it was, many believe, a deliberate policy action by one player, Saudi Arabia, to manipulate the market. And if Saudi Arabia alone could depress prices, then Saudi Arabia could raise prices too.

This perception came to the forefront when Saudi King Abdullah bin Abdulaziz Al Saud died in late January 2015. His death prompted this analysis from CNBC on January 22: "While the short-term plan [of Saudi Arabia] is likely to attempt to hurt frackers, Iran, and Russia via an over-supplied market, the longer-term implications are for oil supply policies that are more hostile toward western consumers." Namely, higher oil prices, in other words.

Indeed the initial reaction to King Abdullah's death was a short-term rise in oil prices. But while the price for Brent, the global oil benchmark, rose as much as 2.5 percent after the king's death was announced, a Newsmax Finance story immediately after the announcement summed up the circumstances by noting that the king's successor, Crown Prince Salman bin Abdulaziz Al Saud, had delivered a speech defending the Saudis and their decision not to decrease oil production despite a drop in prices. The Newsmax story noted, "That was a clear signal to everyone . . . that the Crown Prince was on board with the policy and isn't going to change."

It was estimated in early 2015 that Saudi Arabia needed oil at $80 a barrel to be able to balance its budget. And with King Abdullah gone, the country was expected to ramp up its cold war against Iran and its proxies in the Middle East. Some of the smaller oil-producing nations in the Middle East did not have the currency reserves that Saudi Arabia had. And no one was certain if the Saudi stance was a ploy or a long-term position to keep oil prices low.

For Newsvestors this required sorting through the evidence and balancing the weight of the arguments and evidence over the potential rise or fall in oil prices on a daily basis.

This points to the fact that often alert and informed Newsvestors can also sometimes make money based on the short-term performance of a stock. Oil can be a complex and volatile stock to own, as its price depends on many factors. Newsvestors have to keep their eye on everything, including geopolitical instability.

Oil supply and prices proved so complex an issue that it became a bouncing ball about which experts from all areas of the investment, geopolitical, and energy worlds could not reach consensus, even as the first quarter of 2015 came to an end.

But for vigilant Newsvestors, the time period between late 2014 and late spring of 2015 turned into a comfortable opportunity to build wealth by following the bouncing ball of oil-related news.

During the first four months of 2015, online, cable, and network broadcast news and financial programs and print sources carried endless headlines and opinions, many of which were contradictory. To understand them, Newsvestors would have first needed to consult a website such as Investpedia.com, which explains the various oil benchmarks:

> There are literally dozens of different oil benchmarks, with each one representing crude oil from a particular part of the globe. However, the price of most of them are pegged to one of three primary benchmarks:

Brent Blend: Roughly two-thirds of all crude contracts around the world reference Brent Blend, making it the most widely used marker of all. These days, "Brent" actually refers to oil from four different fields in the North Sea: Brent, Forties, Oseberg, and Ekofisk. Crude from this region is light and sweet, making them ideal for the refining of diesel fuel, gasoline and other high-demand products. And because the supply is waterborne, it's easy to transport to a distant locations.

West Texas Intermediate (WTI): WTI refers to oil extracted from wells in the United States and sent via pipeline to Cushing, Oklahoma. The fact that supplies are landlocked is one of the drawbacks to West Texas crude—it's relatively expensive to ship to certain parts of the globe. The product itself is very light and very sweet, making it ideal for gasoline refining, in particular. WTI continues to be the main benchmark for oil consumed in the United States.

Dubai/Oman: This Middle Eastern crude is a useful reference for oil of a slightly lower grade than WTI or Brent. A "basket" product consisting of crude from Dubai, Oman, or Abu Dhabi, it's somewhat heavier and has higher sulfur content, putting it in the "sour" category. Dubai/Oman is the main reference for Persian Gulf oil delivered to the Asian market.

No one can become an expert overnight in an area as complex as oil trading as a commodity, but Newsvestors, like the competitive academic debater or law student preparing for an exam, need only have a slightly deeper knowledge than that of the average consumer of news. Newsvestors follow the news stories and learn quickly to follow the ups and downs of a stock or commodity as it applies to the flow of news.

In early January, a *Wall Street Journal* headline announced "Oil Prices Tumble to Fresh Lows." A week later, a *Washington Post* blog asked, "How Low Can Oil Go?" For true Newsvestors, there was no certain answer, but one thing was for sure: production had been cut back throughout the United States.

READ, READ, READ

To truly get a handle on such a complicated issue, Newsvestors are often smart to seek out more industry intensive and less mainstream news sources. Consider this lengthy but instructive segment at the beginning of March 2015 in the online site Oilprice.com:

> After tanking to a low of $44 per barrel in January, falling rig counts and enormous reductions in exploration budgets have fueled speculation that the market will correct sometime later this year.
>
> However, there is a possibility that the recent rise to $51 for WTI and $60 for Brent may only be temporary. In fact, several trends are conspiring to force prices down for a second time.
>
> Drillers are consciously deciding to delay the completion of their wells, holding off in hopes that oil prices will rebound, according to E&E's EnergyWire. The decision to put well completions on hold could provide a critical boost to the ultimate profitability of many projects. Higher oil prices in

the months ahead will provide companies with more money for each barrel sold. But also, with the bulk of a given shale well's lifetime production coming within the first year or two, it becomes all the more important to bring a well online when oil prices are favorable. With prices still depressed—WTI is hovering just above $50 per barrel—drillers are waiting for sunnier days.

Yet another reason to wait is the possibility that costs for well completions will decline. Oil and gas companies often contract out well completions to third parties, and those companies will face pressure to cut their fees in order to keep business. That works in favor of producers who put their projects on hold for the time being. Well completions can make up as much as three-quarters of the total project cost.

Several prominent shale drillers have confirmed they are undertaking such a wait-and-see strategy.

And a double dip was exactly what occurred. By March 6, 2015, Reuters reported that oil had suffered its biggest drop since January. Suddenly it was clear that oil prices, and thus solid oil-related companies, were not as much a falling knife as they were a bouncing ball.

So the question arose, how do Newsvestors gain the confidence to determine oil, in general, and companies such as ConocoPhillips and Exxon Mobile to be bouncing balls rather than falling knives?

In the latter part of 2014, as oil prices were not only dropping but making headlines, plenty of news stories pointed out that companies related to oil production, including fracking, were cutting back their future efforts in a big way. Newsvestors who had the courage to catch the knife early in October 2014 bought ConocoPhillips shares at around $63. If they monitored the news and watched, they had at least three opportunities to sell those same shares at over $70. Or if they were buying the dips, they had opportunities to purchase more shares at nearly $60 a share and dollar average their way to a comfortable position that could create a major long-term gain months, if not years, later.

As a dedicated Newsvestor, I chose to treat the oil plunge and the bouncing ball as trading opportunities. I set my own range, with $60 appearing as the support level or bottoming-out price that I was comfortable with for shares of ConocoPhillips. I artificially set the high-water mark in late 2014 at $70 a share. That seemed to be the range of its highs and lows through all manner of news stories. Anything under $60 a share would have forced me to rethink my strategy of perhaps buying more shares to dollar average the stock at a lower rate. It would have been risky to push beyond the $70 point. But I enjoyed ConocoPhillips's generous dividend for several quarters and had the ability to sell each time at the higher end of the range. The Newsvesting rule here was to create an acceptable trading range and stick to it.

In reality, some purchases I made were in the $63–$65 dollar range and most sells were at the $67 or slightly above level. But over the period from the early fall of 2014 to the end of the first quarter of 2015, the opportunity to book a good $4–$5 profit on shares of ConocoPhillips arose numerous times.

I guess the theory that the oil glut would not last forever and that prices would continue to fluctuate and rise, at least during the first quarter of 2015, came from the evidence I collected related to the reaction to the oversupply. The *Wall Street Journal* reported in late January 2015 that "Oil Jumps as Number of Drilling Rigs Drops." The story noted:

> U.S. oil prices surged 8.3% as traders jettisoned bearish bets against the market after data showed a steep drop in the number of rigs drilling for oil in the country—a sign that crude production may be starting to ebb.

I turned to an industry insider news source. At about the same time the *WSJ* story appeared, a story on Oilprice.com proclaimed, "Increased Demand for Refined Products Will Increase Oil Prices." Here are parts of the analysis:

> Keep in mind that oil production is also going to drop in response to lower prices. The U.S. active drilling rig count dropped by another 43 for the week ending January 23, 2015, to 1,633. Based on the upstream companies' capital budgets . . . expect the active rig count to drop below 1,000 by the end of May. We will soon have less than 700 rigs drilling for oil in this country and that means U.S. oil production will be on decline by the 4th quarter. In the last three

years, only the U.S., Canada and Brazil have increased production. The rest of the world's oil production has been in decline despite previous $100/bbl oil prices.

The analysis continued:

In my opinion, within six months the rate of demand growth will accelerate to over 2 million barrels per day. Demand could go even higher if consumers adjust their driving habits like they did back in 1986.

Of course there were plenty of stories to keep Newsvestors on edge even as oil prices appeared to rebound a bit during the early spring of 2015. Consider the April 7, 2015, MarketWatch online story that stated:

While noting that a decline in U.S. rig count has been faster than expected, that reduction is still not enough to change the course of the oil market, they said in a report dated Monday.

"It remains insufficient in our view to balance the U.S. market in 2016," they said. "Prices need to stay low for longer to achieve a sufficient and sustainable slowdown in U.S. production growth."

Goldman Sachs has forecast that crude oil will trade around $40 a barrel over the next three months, although it has noted there is "modest upside" to that prediction—that is, there's a risk prices could be higher.

Newsvestors needed to balance the facts (evidence) and issues at this point. The level of U.S. production, pegged as the culprit in this ongoing oil glut, had been reduced substantially, even shocking the experts at Goldman Sachs. And there was little evidence to sustain the position that oil would trade around $40 a barrel from April through June 2015. The trends and evidence didn't back the Goldman Sachs short-term projections.

In other words, the balance of evidence suggested that U.S. oil production had declined, and the price of oil would be closer to the $60 level by June. Prudent Newsvesting requires taking all of the evidence, balancing it, determining which arguments are most persuasive, and making a decision.

Anyone who actually followed the Goldman projections would have seen little opportunity to buy a stock such as ConocoPhillips. But with shares closing at $64.81 the day after the Goldman story, it seemed another run closer to the higher end of the $60 range was in order. Within a month, ConocoPhillips closed numerous times above $68 and even above $69. This as the rest of the stock market was feeling heat from weak economic news.

There were two choices for Newsvestors, and either would have been reasonable. The first would have been to hold on to ConocoPhillips and ExxonMobil as long-term potential home-run winners. That would make the Goldman analysis and others like it irrelevant. The other would be to sell the stock as it crossed the $68 level and wait for another likely bounce downward of a ball that likely was headed up.

I chose to take my investments out of ConocoPhillips in early May 2015 but to keep my Exxon holdings in place. In reality, ConocoPhillips was down less for FY 2015 at the end of the first quarter. But ExxonMobil (XOM) had less exposure to the ups and downs of exploration, would likely lift as gas prices rose, and paid a great dividend. Most analysts rated the stock as a buy or a hold.

But with analysts just as high, if not higher, on ConocoPhillips, I knew that once it started heading toward the mid-to-low $60 range, I would likely purchase it again. I would either be catching a falling knife that I would later dollar average as it kept falling for a longer-term of ownership or be following the bouncing ball, expecting it to rebound again for another sale.

Newsvesting goes that way. You buy good companies with the understanding you might be holding them for many years. But if you find a great bouncing ball, and evidence supports your belief that it can continue to bounce, you perform like any good news cycle—you come and you go and you come back again.

ANOTHER PLAYER IN THE PIPELINE

The oil glut was not the only play on energy during the latter part of 2014. Newsvestors should always keep a keen eye on related areas once something as big as the price of oil becomes an issue.

Just as prevalent as the oil glut was, the equally (if not more) impressive oversupply and decreasing price of natural gas was also newsworthy. Since 2008, the price of natural gas has steeply declined. For example, residential price per thousand cubic feet in July 2008 was $20.77; in February 2015, it was $9.10. And commercial prices were even lower. If the oil glut seemed a temporary issue, natural gas and particularly liquefied natural gas (LNG) seemed a hopeless matter to average investors.

A look at the obvious other fuel in late 2014 provides a very quick and clear overview. While natural gas prices were low in the United States, they were outrageously high in Europe and China (hundreds of dollars per thousand cubic feet was not uncommon) and other places. Many countries in Western Europe, news sources revealed, were dependent on Russia for their natural gas. And Russia was playing hardball.

Newsvestors who looked into the price of gas, with a broad search term, likely found stories about both oil and natural gas. While examining more industry intensive news sources, Newsvestors would have found stories such as this in Oilprice.com in early 2015:

> It is not as if China's LNG demand is in freefall. Still, China's LNG consumption is growing much slower than anticipated. "The expansion of China's gas supply infrastructure has outpaced the development of gas utilization," Wang Zimeng, an analyst from Sublime China Information, told Interfax. In short, China is finishing off LNG import terminals but doesn't need all the gas that those ports can handle.
>
> Meanwhile, a dramatic development is underway in Europe, where LNG shippers are suddenly seeing surging demand for LNG. Europe is now actually surpassing Asia to become the strongest LNG market in the world.

Such stories were abundant even as 2014 came to an end. That begged the question, which company has an advantage in the natural gas (primarily now traded as liquefied natural gas) business when it comes to the U.S. market?

In late 2014 and early 2015, numerous news searches related to LNG and natural gas showed the same results: the pivotal company was Golar. Here's an example from January 2015 in MarketWatch:

> Golar LNG Limited (Golar LNG) announced agreement

with Singapore's Keppel Shipyard Limited (Keppel) for conversion of the 125,000 m3 LNG carrier Golar Gimi to a floating liquefaction facility (FLNGV).

Golar LNG Partners LP (Golar LNG Partners) has signed an agreement to acquire the ownership interests in the companies that will own and operate the Golar Eskimo, a floating storage and regasification unit, from Golar LNG Limited for an aggregate purchase price of c. $390.0 million.

Is your head spinning? Mine was. This is when having an investment advisor with significant resources and experience is immensely valuable. Having seen Golar pop up over and over again, I asked my advisor about the LNG space. His research showed Golar LNG surfacing repeatedly.

The reasoning was the same as that stated by another investment firm:

Golar LNG Ltd (GLNG), based out of London, is a liquefied natural gas (LNG) shipping company. The research note by Citigroup Inc. Research Equities, released on December 31, last year, reiterates a Buy rating as the company announced an agreement with Keppel Corporation Limited (ADR) to convert one of its LNG carriers, Gimi, into a Floating Liquefaction Vessel (FLNGV). It is the second such vessel, set for conversion, and shows commitment on part of Golar to its long-term vision of leading the floating liquefaction market.

According to Citi analyst Christian Wetherbee, this is a huge positive, as Golar is lining up FLNGV opportunities for itself, which could trigger growth in the company's earnings and cash flows.

"Citi analysts have reiterated a Buy rating on the stock," he said, "with a price target of $66, representing 89.6% upside potential."

As mentioned, the Golar LNG example is a great one to illustrate why working with a trustworthy investment professional is so important to the process of Newsvesting. I knew I was interested in the crush on oil prices, and that led to a general discussion of related commodities and stocks.

That, in turn, led to my financial advisor alerting me to Golar, which I was already somewhat familiar with. Long story short, I made an investment in Golar several times in early 2015, both at around the $31–$32 range and at the $35 level. By early May 2015, Golar shares had risen to well over $47 per. Not knowing this business as well as I would like, I chose to take the substantial profits (34 percent on various purchases made over a six-month period) from the sale of Golar shares in order to clear some additional cash. That was in preparation of the likely change in interest rates and the potential impact on the market in the coming year. But Golar was a great short-term gain.

One thing Newsvestors should know: if something rises that quickly, take your profits and move on! The short-term investment in Golar resulted in a nice return in less than four months. That also included a dividend paid out during that time.

Better to make a profit on a solid Newsvestment and move on if you are in an area where you still feel somewhat uncertain or one that turns out not to be a passion. I had no real passion for following Golar. So I remembered Julius Caesar's succinct synopsis in his *Commentaries on the Gallic War*: Veni, vidi, vici—I came, I saw, I conquered—and I was out.

ISSUE 8 Oil Prices Begin to Decline Early into 2014

INITIAL EVIDENCE

March 29, 2014, Barron's: "The long-term outlook for global oil prices is lower, perhaps much lower."

June 9, 2014, Forbes: "9 Reasons Why Oil Process May Be Headed for a Bust."

October 15, 2014: "Global Oil Glut Sends Prices Plunging."

EXTENDED EVIDENCE

December 8, 2014: Seeking Alpha, "Crude Oil: A Bounce Is on the Horizon."

January 2015, *the Wall Street Journal*: "Oil Jumps as Number of Drilling Rigs Drops . . . U.S. oil prices surged 8.3 percent."

January 20, 2015, *USA Today*: "former CEO . . . Shell Oil . . . next round of high prices likely to start later (in 2015)."

March 2015, Oilprice.com: "Recent rise to $51 for WTI and $60 Brent may be temporary . . . trends are conspiring to force prices down a second time."

ISSUE 9 LNG (Liquified Natural Gas) Demand in China Goes into Decline in 2014

INITIAL EVIDENCE

February 2015, Hellenic Shipping News: "China's LNG Imports Continue to Stagnate."

January 2015, Oilprice.com: "LNG are suddenly seeing surging demands in Europe."

January 2015, MarketWatch.com: "Golar LNG to acquire ownership in floating liquefaction facility."

EXTENDED EVIDENCE

May 5, 2015, Investor's.com: "Golar LNG (NASDAQ:GLNG) shares soared Tuesday after it said it began talks to order another liquefied natural gas vessel and said it was named a partner for a project in Equatorial Guinea."

ISSUE 8 Oil Prices Begin to Decline Early into 2014

ANALYSIS

Crude oil prices were dropping long before most mainstream media sources were reporting the drop. Oil is supply and demand. Behavior of prices in the last quarter of 2014 looked like a "bouncing ball" and would likely continue that pattern into the second quarter of 2015. Decision to invest in strong dividend/yield companies. Choose one refinery and one oil petrochemical production company and trade on the "bouncing ball." Choices are Exxon Mobil (XOM) and ConocoPhillips (COP). Both have strong dividend/yield. COP bounces more like a ball.

CONCLUSION/ACTION

Purchased Conoco-Phillips (COP) between $60 and $65 in late 2014 and early 2015 Also purchased Exxon-Mobil during a dip in October of 2015.

RESULT

Sold various positions in COP in the first quarter of 2015 with an average profit of $3-to-$4. Held XOM through Newsvesting period. Purchased more COP and XOM when prices plunged in August of 2015 with idea to purchase more if prices dropped substantially in the future.

ISSUE 9 LNG (Liquified Natural Gas) Demand in China Goes into Decline in 2014

ANALYSIS

Golar (GLNG) was uniquely situated to meet Europe's growing demand for LNG in a rapidly changing set of circumstances.

CONCLUSION/ACTION

Purchased GLNG in December of 2014 at $35.71 a share.

RESULT

Sold GLNG in May 2015 for $47.59 (33.75% return in five months).

CHAPTER **10**

When Everyone's Happy, Caveat Emptor!

BUYER (AND SELLER) BEWARE

Nothing brings out more argumentative, nerdy, authoritative know-it-alls than the world of pollsters—the so-called experts who critique their work or convert it into statistical models for the purpose of predicting results.

In my years as chairman of a company that provided political and issue-related polling to news organizations, we conducted surveys that were right on the money and others that seemingly missed the mark. My measure of success was always how close our last survey was to the final results in a major political contest—and did we show the ultimate winner leading.

In good years, like the 2008 presidential contest, when we were polling for the political news organization Politico, the results were pretty darn good. The editors at Politico asked us to poll the presidential contest based on certain swing counties in what were considered swing states. While one might think polling a state is harder than a county, in a presidential contest, it's actually a bigger pain to poll just one county because finding enough respondents to have a strong sample and to continue to track their sentiments through the election takes a major effort. You can run out of voters willing to answer your survey.

But our results were strong that year. In reality, and contrary to popular opinion, most public opinion research firms, those who poll for news organizations or academic institutions and not for particular political parties or candidates, are very accurate. That's especially true considering they must take surveys where the turnout levels at the polls of varying ages, races, and political affiliations, as well the percentage of male versus female voters, must be predicted or weighed to balance out over- or undersampling of these various demographic groups.

And for broadcast or print pollsters, there can be no pushing of a respondent to a poll, forcing them to make a choice between candidates on a ballot. Thus, most nonpartisan polls will still have a certain percentage of undecided voters, even a day or so before the election.

Added to this complicated mix is the growing use of cell phones that substitute for land lines and increased reliance on the Web for communication. Polls now have to gather their responses from all of these modes of communication, particularly if they want to attract the opinion of younger adults.

The RealClearPolitics.com (RCP) average of all national surveys for the 2012 presidential contest ended with Barack Obama leading Mitt Romney with 48.8 percent of the vote to Romney's 48.1 percent, with the remaining 3 percent or so either undecided or voting for a third party. That may seem way off when one considers the final national vote outcome of 51.1 percent for Obama and 47.2 percent for Romney. But in reality it was highly accurate. And the answer to why it was accurate explains why opinion research and polling remains both a science and an art, important to understanding how the public views both political candidates as well as other issues, such as the economy.

The polls that made up the RCP national presidential polling average all had margins of error attached to their surveys. The margin of error is not some whimsical number pulled out of thin air by a pollster who declares, "I think I may be off by three points." Instead, it is the maximum expected difference between the true population parameter and the sample population gathered in a survey. There are specific formulas that establish the margin of error for scientific polls. In the instance of the 2012 presidential race, most of the national polls utilized in creating the RealClearPolitics average had margins of error of plus or minus 3 percent.

That meant that the 2012 polls, when aggregated and averaged, were well within their margin of error and showed President Obama, when rounded off, with a one-point lead over Mitt Romney at the end. And in most cases, the polls related to the 2014 elections for the U.S. Senate in various states had similar results.

When one thinks about the complexity of asking a few thousand people, who are meant to be representative of tens of millions of voters, about who they will vote for and managing to come in with numbers even close to being correct, it's rather stunning.

All of that is to say that while the pundits and experts love to pick on polls and pollsters, the fact remains that the data they provide tends to be extremely reliable. But when it comes to Newsvesting, how is that data of any real assistance?

WHEN SURVEYS MEAN MORE THAN JUST NUMBERS

Looking at numerous long-standing surveys of the American public concerning views about the economy, attitudes as consumers, and likely levels of spending, as well as opinions on whether the nation as a whole is headed in the right or wrong direction, there seems little that would at first glance provide much guidance as to where the economy, much less the various financial markets, is headed in the future. However, there are a few long-standing and highly credible national surveys that may be predictive of future economic dips.

The research firm Opinion Savvy looked at the Michigan Survey of Consumer Sentiment Index, which was created by professor George Katona at the University of Michigan's Institute for Social Research in the 1940s. Like many surveys, it is conducted by phone and is designed to capture views of the economy and personal spending sentiments of a cross section of U.S. consumers each month.

Most financial experts and economists view this index, which has become one of the major accepted surveys by which to measure the U.S. economy, as a good measure of where our economy is and where it is headed. The index rises as consumers gain increased confidence in the economy and when the respondents to the survey express, through a series of questions, an increased likelihood to increase their spending in general.

Traditionally, as the index rises, prices for shares in car manufacturers, home builders, and retail companies rise. And it is also true that the value of the dollar tends to fluctuate with the index. When it's higher, the dollar is also.

But if surveys could predict the future of the economy or the markets, then it wouldn't be all that difficult for anyone to invest and make money.

The problem is that the market has often already risen by the time the index is released.

I don't advocate that Newsvestors pore over endless public opinion surveys about whether the country is going in what direction or to what degree the public is pleased with the economy. And I don't believe that surveys can guide immediate investment strategies. Yes, there are many who believe we can review various long-standing surveys and find patterns that can indeed steer investment moves. But surveys and public polls are complicated enough to understand when taken one at a time. And trying to examine multiple surveys and how they intersect to suggest economic or investment opportunities poses a nearly impossible challenge.

There is, however, a potential role surveys can play in helping us decide to at least evaluate the degree to which Newsvestors are invested in equities versus moving more resources to cash.

The Michigan Consumer Sentiment Index is readily available through a simple web search and has been consistent for years. In April 2015 I examined the Opinion Savvy analysis of the index in my column. Here's how the story ran on Newsmax.com on April 23:

> Every week I read stories about how the stock market is going to crash and our economy will soon melt down in a more dramatic manner than it did in late 2007. I generally dismiss these as just one person's opinion, backed up by convoluted assumptions.
>
> And let me be clear, I am not suggesting that such a meltdown is imminent. But a study from the research firm Opinion Savvy gives real cause to wonder if the wild bull run on Wall Street might finally be coming to an end later this year.
>
> The so-called economic recovery we have "enjoyed" has been less than even-handed. Corporate CEOs and the Wall Street crowd managed to make a post–Great Recession comeback with even bigger salaries and more money feeding into their investment world. For the average American, however, wages have hardly budged.
>
> Unemployment, at least officially, has dropped to more than acceptable levels; that is, unless you are one of the

multitude of people who has given up searching for a job or who took a lower-paying one to make ends meet.

Corporate earnings for the last quarter so far are mixed, and the stock market is lurching from huge gains one day and huge losses the next. And it seems just a bit of good news, like the boost in the sale of existing houses for March, leads people to conclude, "Things must be better, at least compared to a few years ago."

And that's where the Opinion Savvy research delivers what could be some daunting news to the investment world.

Since 1978, the University of Michigan has conducted their Survey of Consumers, which includes what they term the "Index of Consumer Sentiment." While no one survey or poll can guarantee a projection into the future, the research produced suggests that this particular index, if used as a quarterly measurement, often is a precursor to downward shifts in the stock market.

The Opinion Savvy study states, "While opinion usually follows the economy, at some points over the past 40 years, opinion has outpaced the market." The study adds that, "When this happens, it seems to spell disaster."

Ouch!

While this conclusion might engage in a bit of hyperbole, the graphs and charts and numbers they provide are fairly convincing that, at the very least, when the Michigan Index of Consumer Sentiment climbs really high, the financial markets in the U.S. decline in the ensuing months.

What gets one's attention is that the index had reached a nearly off-the-charts high by the end of the second quarter in 2007. We all know what followed just months later as our financial institutions started to go into a near-death spiral and the economy followed with the Great Recession, which about did us in.

The real shocker is that this same index is now at its highest level since those chart-busting early days of 2007. While the Opinion Savvy chart for the most recent data ends with data from the end of 2014, the research report states that the index has climbed from a score in the low 80s in the last quarter of 2014 to a current index number of 96. The study focuses on the index number reported for the first month of each quarter. That means April's number is perilously close to the 97 score that was reported in early 2007.

The same report is quick to note that there is no causal relationship between the Michigan Index and the U.S. equity markets. But they make a strong case that when sentiment is rocketing up the chart, markets drop, often substantially, within a matter of months, not years, thereafter.

Their same analysis showed sentiment at an all-time high before the Dot-com bubble burst of 2000 and the same correlation with the post-9/11 recession.

The good news for investors is that the Michigan index is not percentile-based and a score can go well above 100. So there is more room for sentiment to rise. The bad news is, it's on the move, which could signal interesting times to come. Is America about to see a post–"Quantitative Easing" bubble burst, bringing the markets down as a result?

Was this column predictive? Did it mean that the economy and the financial markets were about to start declining? Not necessarily. But it did warrant examination. And among the surveys that were consistent and used by both the media and economists, it seemed, as the Opinion Savvy firm's examination suggested, the most evident and available chart had seemingly crested right before major declines in the economy and hence the markets.

The Opinion Savvy survey was based on the April Michigan Index of Consumer sentiment. And if the analysis of the index was not a warning that the economy could be in trouble in the long run, it was a very good warning of a speed bump in the road—right ahead of us.

The first quarter of 2015 was filled with tough weather and some major labor strikes. Still, this *Wall Street Journal* headline for April 29 took many by surprise: "U.S. Economic Growth Nearly Stalls Out: Businesses Slash Investment, Exports Tumble and Consumers Show Caution as GDP

Expands at 0.2% Pace."

The *Wall Street Journal* story reported a bleak version of the quarter that had seen the Michigan Index zoom to some of its highest levels since before the start of the financial meltdown of late 2007 and the Great Recession that followed:

> The U.S. economy slowed to a crawl at the start of the year as businesses slashed investment, exports tumbled and consumers showed signs of caution, marking a return to the uneven growth that has been a hallmark of the nearly six-year economic expansion.
>
> Gross domestic product, the broadest measure of goods and services produced across the economy, expanded at a 0.2% seasonally adjusted annual rate in the first quarter, the Commerce Department said Wednesday. The economy advanced at a 2.2% pace in the fourth quarter and 5% in the third.

Then came a Reuters report on May 13:

> U.S. business inventories barely rose in March . . . the latest indication that the economy actually contracted in the first quarter.
>
> The Commerce Department said on Wednesday business inventories edged up 0.1 percent after a downwardly revised 0.2 percent gain in February. Inventories are a key component of gross domestic product.
>
> Retail inventories excluding autos, which go into the calculation of GDP, ticked up 0.1 percent in March. That was well below the 0.8 percent gain the government assumed in its advance estimate of first-quarter growth published last month.
>
> That was the latest suggestion that first-quarter GDP growth could be revised down from the scant 0.2 percent annual pace reported in April to show a contraction.

Then came a May 18 report in BusinessInsider.com with the headline:

"Homebuilder Sentiment Fell More than Expected in May":

> The National Association of Homebuilders' index fell to
> 54 last month. Economists had forecast a rise to 57 from 56
> the previous month, according to Bloomberg. The associa-
> tion noted that despite the drop, the index is still above the
> 50-point benchmark. "Consumers are exhibiting caution,
> and want to be on more stable financial footing before pur-
> chasing a home," said NAHB chief economist David Crowe.

It appeared that regardless of any long-term validity to the Opinion
Savvy analysis of the Michigan Index, there was certainly a reason to believe that when the index usually shot above a score of 95 on its scale,
one could anticipate a cooling in economic reports. But how could
Newsvestors even begin to anticipate the quarter's GDP report by the federal government?

NEWSVESTING TO NOWCASTING:
THE SECRET OF THE ATLANTA FED

Newsvestors might be wise to pay attention to another process that
sounds a bit like Newsvesting. It's called Nowcasting. Jon Hartley, a contributor to *Forbes*, explained following the weak GDP numbers for early
2015:

> This week, the 2015 first quarter GDP growth . . . came
> in well below the expected 1.0% consensus forecast among
> Wall Street analysts. However, an innovative forecasting
> tool pioneered by economists at the Atlanta Fed was nearly
> spot on, forecasting 0.1% growth. GDPNow is a real-time
> GDP forecasting methodology that sources data from previ-
> ous months which has already been released, and attempts
> to predict using this data what GDP number the already
> available data implies. . . . This methodology, commonly re-
> ferred to as "Nowcasting," takes advantage of the fact that
> GDP is released at nearly a month lag from quarter-end,
> weeks after the final jobs report for the last month of the

quarter is released. It's become an increasingly popular trend to "nowcast" key economic indicators like GDP.

Everybody familiar with the rudiments of our economic system knows the Federal Reserve System is headed by the Federal Reserve Board (or board of governors), headquartered in Washington DC. But the real nitty-gritty of the Fed is the bankers' banks that make up the Federal Reserve Bank as a whole, namely, the twelve regional reserve banks (such as Atlanta) across the country. In addition to "storing currency and coin, and processing checks and electronic payments, Reserve Banks also supervise commercial banks in their regions," according to Federalreserveeducation.org. "As the bank for the U.S. government, Reserve Banks handle the Treasury's payments, sell government securities and assist with the Treasury's cash management and investment activities." And here's perhaps the most poignant part of their role as it relates to Newsvesting: "Reserve Banks conduct research on regional, national and international economic issues. Research plays a critical role in bringing broad economic perspectives to the national policymaking arena."

In other words, the regional reserve banks are tasked with having their collective ears to the ground at all times. They funnel information to the board that then sets national economic policies, affecting all of us.

In his *Forbes* article, Hartley noted:

> According to the Wall Street Journal, a number of Wall Street economists have increasingly started tracking the Atlanta Fed GDPNow methodology, citing economists like Eric Green from TD Securities, who follow the index closely. . . . He reported that as of early May the Atlanta Fed's GDP-Now is already predicting a GDP shortfall in the second quarter of 2015. According to the Atlanta Fed, "The initial GDPNow model forecast for real GDP growth (seasonally adjusted annual rate) in the second quarter of 2015 was 0.9 percent on April 30." This is somewhat higher than the first quarter forecast of 0.1 percent, but would still be a surprising indication of continued weakness, should the official estimate from the Bureau of Economic Analysis fall in that neighborhood, well below the historical real GDP growth

rate of 3 percent for the greater part of the 20th century postwar period.

To Newsvestors, the Atlanta Fed's Nowcast could become increasingly important in the future. The *Forbes* report noted the GDPNow forecast becomes incredibly accurate within one month of the release of the official GDP figures from the Bureau of Economic Analysis, once the jobs report for the final month of the quarter is released, supplying the last piece of the puzzle for the GDPNow forecasting methodology.

But before the Atlanta Fed forecast could or should become a mandatory staple for Newsvesting, there had to be closure on a controversy that likely would not be resolved before the late spring of 2015. Economists at the San Francisco Fed posted an economic letter suggesting that the official GDP growth announced by the government was likely off.

Writing for TheStreet.com, economist Roger Arnold noted:

> In the letter, economists from the [San Francisco] bank claimed that first quarter gross domestic product was substantially higher than reported by the U.S. Department of Commerce's Bureau of Economic Analysis in the Advance Estimate provided on April 29. . . . The BEA announced that the annualized rate of GDP growth expansion was 0.2%, which is almost exactly what the Federal Reserve Bank of Atlanta forecasted with the bank's GDPNow model.

The justification for the San Francisco Fed's dispute, according to Arnold, was that the average first quarter GDP growth rates of the past sixteen years had been lower than that of the 1980s and 1990s, and after applying a "residual seasonality" adjustment to account for this, the first quarter GDP growth rate for 2015 moved to a positive 1.8%.

Arnold went on to shred the San Francisco Fed letter to pieces, providing extremely detailed analysis that, in essence, argued there was no seasonal aberration in 2015 that could account for such a massive mistake.

BusinessInsider.com likely summed up the situation best:

> Here's Deutsche Bank's Jim Reid in a note to clients on Wednesday: "We started the week speculating that it's

possible (although not the most likely scenario) that the US economy may have shrunk in H1 2015. 48 hours later and we've seen the San Fran Fed paper on faulty Q1 seasonals gather traction and yesterday we saw blockbuster housing starts and permits so perhaps we're actually in boom time?" Reid, however, isn't so sure it's time to "crack open the champagne" because, well, the Atlanta Fed's number didn't change at all after the housing data.

Newsvestors caught in the middle of such data could surmise several things. First, the actual GDP for the first quarter of 2015 could possibly be revised upward down the road. Second, it would be unlikely not to see the second quarter's GDP substantially higher given that a quick look into past GDP numbers would suggest that first quarter GDP growth numbers are usually weaker. If we take the much higher GDP numbers produced by the San Francisco crowd or the much lower official percentage (and that of the Atlanta Fed), add them and divide the result by two, the number would not have been what most economists expected.

Whether the Atlanta Fed model would hold as predictive of a much weaker economy in the entire first half of 2015 remained to be seen. But as various components of its forecast began to reveal themselves, Newsvestors could follow the news stories that related to those numbers and begin to search for new opportunities to invest or to sell. Consider this ChristainScienceMonitor.com story that appeared in online news reports about the retail sales report:

> US retail sales were flat in April, according to the Commerce Department. Consumers simply aren't parting with their money as easily as they used to, which has left one segment of the retail industry reeling: stores in or near America's shopping malls.

The alarming news about these malls could have created a new issue for anyone interested in Newsvesting in or out of companies or related industries that might be impacted by this stark report, which went on to explain:

Once the central nervous system of shopping in America, traditional indoor malls (along with all retail spaces) have seen their foot traffic take a nosedive over the last five years. Analysts estimate that half of US malls will close over the next two decades, as consumers increasingly choose to shop online.

MOVING TO HIGHER GROUND

Regardless of which side was right in the battle of the GDP calculation—the Atlanta Fed or San Francisco Fed—the official GDP number announced in late April 2015 brought out endless stories about distressed segments of the economy, and the decline of malls was worthy of creating a new issue for Newsvesting.

It didn't take much to realize that the mall story was real. And it took even less time to enter a web search with the phrase "malls surviving while others close" to learn who the winner in this decline would likely be. One name popped up: Simon.

Consider this from a Wharton School of Business post:

> While upscale malls like many of those operated by Simon are likely to attract visitors and retailers for the foreseeable future, it's unclear what will happen to the "B" and "C" malls. "While we expect some retailers to close stores in the competitive retail environment, there is a long list of domestic and international retailers looking for space in high-productivity malls and . . . Simon Property Group will backfill any closures relatively quickly," Nathan Isbee, an analyst at investment firm Stifel, said in a research note. "Simon will view any store closures as an opportunity to mark rents to market and sign a lease with a stronger retailer."

Sure enough, additional research proved that to be true. Simon Property Group Inc. (SPG) reached a low of around $162 a share in October 2014 and then saw its shares soar to $206 in January 2015. As 2015 progressed, it bounced between a $190 ceiling and a support area of around $180. If the entire market were overpriced, then Simon would likely take a bath with all the other pricey stocks down the road. But remembering the rule that investments should be made on a long-term basis, Simon seemed to have the very best malls with high-end tenants who could withstand a downturn in the economy. They jumped my Newsvesting flow sheet, particularly given the incredible dividend yield of over 3 percent.

And while numbers released in early summer of 2015 suggested that spending was up and that the cold winter of 2015's freeze on the economy was thawing, the direction consumers would take in the next few years was up in the air. Would a rate hike down the road by the Fed freeze economic growth? Would the public hold on to its money as rates increased?

That was all up in the air. But one thing that was established during both the tech bubble burst and the Great Recession was the fact that high-end retail, along with the lower end of the retail business, tends not to suffer as much as retailers selling somewhere in the middle as to price and quality.

So Simon Property Group would be an investment in the long term, and I was prepared to purchase it at various increments should it fall in the coming months or years. I was sure it would survive and flourish down the road.

The overall GDP controversy led to Newsvesting that came from numerous topics and issues springing out of it.

But in the end, the overriding issue that both the Opinion Savvy analysis of the Michigan Index and the Atlanta Fed's Nowcast presented was a much bigger one. And it was not an issue of jumping out of the markets as much as it was of how far to jump in.

Everyone will tell you that you can't time the market. But in reality, it should be easier to time when to exit equities in favor of a stronger cash position than it is to time when to get or stay in to catch an unexpected bull run.

However, it's often easier to buy stocks than to sell them. Newsvestors must be prepared to do both with equal confidence based on their disciplined approach and the evidence they collect from news, surveys, and opinion stories each and every day.

And make no mistake, for average investors it may sound good to hear that you should stick with stocks and ride out bad times. But when it is all of your savings or when you rely on the value of your portfolio for whatever reason that might be more immediate in nature, such a concept is a bit unrealistic. There are plenty of ways to hedge things in life, including hedging against a major decline in a net worth you have worked to create.

A GREATER CASH POSITION

A FoxBusiness.com story helped set the stage for a Newsvesting issue that had been worth watching for years and was starting to become critical as Americans headed into the summer of 2015. Dunstan Prial reported:

> It takes some digging, but inflation data released Friday [May 22] supports forecasts that the Federal Reserve will start lifting interest rates later this year, possibly as early as September. The key figure is what's known as the core Consumer Price Index, an economic indicator that gauges how much the prices have changed on an array of consumer products excluding food and energy because those costs are often volatile. The core CPI has risen 1.8% in the past 12 months, just below the Fed's target rate of 2%.

For older investors who lived through the Jimmy Carter presidency, the concept of double-digit inflation and high interest rates are either reviled times remembered for the crushing cost of borrowing funds, or alternatively, the glory days. But the only people who remembered those times as glory days are those who owed little and had plenty of cash they could stuff in financial vehicles as simple as money market accounts.

By 1980, taxable money market rates were averaging nearly 13 percent. For those who had held on to their cash and were liquid, money market accounts and secondary market certificate of deposit accounts helped fight high inflation caused in part by an energy crisis, which in all honesty began long before Carter took office.

Of course the prime interest rate charged by banks in 1980 was over 15 percent, and new mortgage rates were sky-high.

The probability that those type of prime interest and mortgage rates or such high returns on low-risk money markets would ever return seemed remote to anyone Newsvesting in 2015 and preparing for an open presidential contest in 2016. And with economic growth seemingly slow and wage growth hardly seeming to catch up to pre–Great Recession levels, it seemed hard to understand why rates should increase and how they would impact a U.S. stock market that had been on its third-longest bull run in history and the economy it allegedly represented. Newsvestors faced one of the great issue analysis challenges ever.

In preparation for that analysis, I moved more of my investment resources to cash. What was left to do was to determine where and when
that cash should be Newsvested in the future and what that near and more
long-term future would look like.

CHAPTER **11**

Future Newsvesting

By late July 2015 there was no question about the reliability of the Atlanta Fed's Nowcast. While most experts on Wall Street had expected the second quarter U.S. GDP to rise at somewhere close to 3 percent, the Nowcast suggested a final number closer to 2.4. (Most of the Wall Street experts had revised their 3 percent prediction down to about 2.6 just days before the actual number was released.) Once again the Nowcast had pegged it.

The report of the improved, if not spectacular, second quarter GDP number, coupled with an upward revision in the first quarter GDP, set the stage for an oh-so-awaited rise in interest rates. Fox Business reported on July 30:

> The Commerce Department on Thursday released its first estimate of second quarter GDP and it wasn't bad: 2.3 percent growth, just short of analysts' estimates of 2.6 percent and a decent rebound from the soft first quarter. A healthy jump in consumer spending was cited as an important catalyst.
>
> But the real news was that first-quarter GDP was once again revised upward, this time to show the economy grew 0.6 percent rather than declining by 0.2 percent. That's a

hugely important distinction—the economy grew in the first quarter, it didn't contract.

The Fox Business story noted, "That distinction is undoubtedly not lost on Federal Reserve policymakers as they mull the timing of the first interest rate hike in nearly a decade."

But news that wages and compensation in the U.S rose only .2 percent for the second quarter had the experts backing off of predictions of an immediate hike in rates. Again, Fox Business reported: "'This report was a bit of a shock since it is not what is expected in a gradually tightening labor market. The central question is whether this very sharp and unexpected decline in wages and salaries will trigger alarm bells at the Fed, causing a delay for the first rate hike,' said Ozlem Yaylaci, an economist with IHS Global Insight." That news, combined with a continued slide in the price of crude oil, led the market to once again slip and slide—and ultimately to continue to trade sideways.

Stocks like Exxon Mobil and ConocoPhillips continued to fall. (ConocoPhillips had lost its safe trading range of between $60 and $70 and found its price closer to $50 a share by late July.) It took discipline to sit out what could be a very long wait before being able to see oil rebound and these companies reach their old highs. But Newsvesting meant buying the strong oil companies with good dividends and yields and averaging down as low as they could go. After all, it was Warren Buffett who made it clear that smart investors buy good companies when others are selling them.

But while most on Wall Street continued to wring their hands, waiting for some sign of when a rate hike would come, some companies and their investors were already entering the future boldly.

FRIENDS IN HIGH PLACES

Boom! It came after my official Newsvesting period for this book elapsed, but on Friday, July 17, another company that had been part of my adventures as a Newsvestor unexpectedly took off and soared. On that day Google gained well over $80 on the day, seeing a 16 percent increase in its share price. By the end of that day the search-engine company turned mobile phone–self-driving car–you-name-it corporation saw its stock (GOOG) become the second most valuable of all U.S. companies.

The news came as the company reported stronger than expected earnings.

More important was when new CFO Ruth Porat suggested that financial discipline for the company and additional return on investment to shareholders were likely in the future.

To illustrate how important Google had become to Newsvestors, consider the headlines of April 14, 2015, when a story broke on virtually every major broadcast and online news site:

> According to the Dow Jones, EU regulators have decided to file formal charges against Google over its search business.
>
> European Union regulators decided Tuesday that they would file charges against Google stemming from an antitrust investigation, multiple news agencies reported.
>
> Citing a source familiar with the matter, the Wall Street Journal reported that the Google decision will be discussed by EU commissioners on Wednesday. That source claimed to the news outlet that European antitrust chief Margrethe Vestager made the decision to file charges after consulting with European Commission President Jean-Claude Juncker.
>
> The Financial Times and The New York Times also reported Tuesday that the EU would accuse the tech giant of abusing its market position, citing sources familiar with the regulators' decision.

The only major news outlet that seemed to ignore this news was Google News, where the headline was marginalized at best. The following day, when the charges were made public, Google News caught up with other media and arguably highlighted the story more than most.

While Google may have seemed under attack, the news leak that the EU could seek billions from the company seemed hardly to affect the Web's biggest fish in after-hours trading that evening. In fact, on the day the charges were officially leveled, Google shares ticked up!

And for anyone who had followed Google's incredible rise and its phenomenal ability to put itself in the right spots politically, there could be little doubt that the company would remain a darling of the investment world for years to come.

Much of that credit goes to the company itself. Very few companies or products enter the lexicon of the public vocabulary by transitioning from the position of being a proper noun to generally accepted verb. Usually technology or business strategy takes a company (such as Xerox) from the once-vaulted status of having people refer to "making a Xerox" of a document to a time when the word turned back into just the name of a once-successful company.

In 2015 it remained likely that in doing a search on the Web, someone was said to have "googled" the subject matter. And in Europe, that was even more likely, given that Google was more of a dominant force among search engines there than it is in the United States.

For Newsvestors who had read countless stories predicting the EU's move, this bump in the company's road created a likely long-run investment opportunity.

Yes, the stock had become incredibly pricey—trading in the $500 to $600 range in the twelve months leading up to the EU announcement. But the advantage that comes from pricey stock is that minor fluctuations, if taken advantage of, can yield substantial dollars.

It would take nearly $5,500 for Newsvestors to own just ten shares in the company. But consider that had Newsvestors purchased those shares at the start of 2015 and sold them at the close of business on the day of the announcement, they would have picked up somewhere north of $33 per share in just four months. Not bad for four months' worth of passive work. And what a four months those were for Google.

Also consider that had the same Newsvestors held the stock through July 17, each share of GOOG would have increased by $148!

The European Union was in a sense somewhat trivial compared to the major issues the company faced in 2014 and early 2015 in the United States. But Google had a little help pursuing its goals. Remember Garth Brooks's song "Friends in Low Places"? In the case of Google, the corporate tune should perhaps be called "Friends in High Places."

With top-level leadership and a brilliant game plan, Google proved that it pays to be friends with a president. Google, to its credit, had joined other major Internet players as strong early supporters of Barack Obama. And that fact wasn't forgotten nor overlooked by Newsvestors.

As mentioned before, Newsvesting sometimes requires reading material that might rile and cause Newsvestors to boycott a company when, instead, they should take the information as a reason to invest in it.

Many conservatives read heavily visited websites such as Townhall.com and RedState.com as sources of legitimate conservative commentary. Those pages are not likely to praise President Obama. Admittedly, my own column has run on Townhall.com for over a decade. Obviously I would tend to agree with much of the commentary on these websites.

But the information picked up on such sites, even by the most conservative of readers, can contribute much to an investment strategy that leads to a very capitalistic reaction: investing in the other side.

Newsvestors who kept up with Google on a regular basis may well have found an article by RedState's front page contributor Ben Howe in early 2013 that expanded on the author's theory that Google had a pattern of helping Democrats, particularly Obama, both with financial contributions as well as helping staff campaigns.

Howe's story was written to counter refutations of an earlier story he had written about the cozy relationship between Google and Obama. In writing about a complicated web of Google connections with the Obama 2012 re-election campaign, he noted:

> The question isn't whether Google collaborates with Democrats, but how Google collaborates with Democrats.
>
> We know that Obama campaign manager Jim Messina received personal mentoring on both technology approaches and management style from Google executive chairman Eric Schmidt, his friend since the 2008 campaign. We know that Google employees overwhelmingly contributed to Democrats in the last cycle (and aggregate individual employee contributions outnumbered the company's PAC contributions). We know that Google vice president and "chief Internet evangelist" Vint Cerf received a presidential appointment to the National Science Board following last year's election.
>
> Is it paranoid to believe that Google is deeply invested in helping Democrats? No.
>
> Still, I decided to take a deeper look at the connections between Google and the Obama campaign.

And so he embarked on that deeper look. While some of the connections required some mental gymnastics, Howe's conclusion that Obama owed much to Team Google, as well as to most of the Silicon Valley crowd, was persuasive. He started with the relationship between Google chairman Eric Schmidt and the Obama campaign.

> Jim Messina called on Google's Eric Schmidt, Apple's Steve Jobs, and Hollywood's Steven Spielberg for their advice on building an organization. Schmidt gave Messina what turned out to be an invaluable piece of advice: "You do not want political people, you want smart people who you are going to draw what you want and they're going to go build it." So Messina went out and hired someone to head the data department who had never worked on a campaign before.
>
> What better pool of talent to draw from than Schmidt's own company? Schmidt himself certainly wasn't shy about being deeply involved with the campaign. He even helped himself to the first slice of a cake, purchased by Obama campaign Dev Ops Director Scott VanDenPlas, emblazoned with "Don't F*ck This Up." Schmidt later told Bloomberg Businessweek that the Obama campaign was the "best-run campaign ever."

From there the article traced one-sided pro-Obama campaign contributions from Google employees to Obama's reelection and so on and so forth. It was enough to infuriate a conservative Republican. But it was also strong enough to convince Newsvestors that whether they liked Google's politics or not, the folks at Google had achieved a rare thing in the world of politics: doing more than just contributing money. After all, plenty of organizations could do that. Instead, Google contributed, directly and indirectly, intellectual capital that was unique and potentially the difference between reelection for Obama or defeat after a seemingly rough four years.

Newsvestors don't have the time or the inclination to get upset about politics while they are Newsvesting. That's saved for when they are not at work. Good Newsvestors would have watched Google's meteoric rise to prominence, their endless diversification of products, and would have started to search for an instance in which their apparent political power might benefit the company and thus shareholders.

In fact, that issue was just around the corner. It was called net neutrality. Just to set a baseline definition for the following discussion, here's how *Business Insider* defined the term in April 2014: "Currently, when you access the internet on your phone, tablet or computer, you get to view websites and watch video at pretty much the same speed everyone else does. The traffic you create simply by browsing the web is treated equally by the companies that have built the infrastructure of the internet—internet service providers (ISPs) like Comcast and AT&T, and 'interconnect' companies like Cogent and Level 3, which route and direct traffic between you and your internet provider. This state of affairs, broadly, is called 'net neutrality.' Everyone gets the same treatment."

Business Insider added that all that was about to change. But first things first.

"AND STILL THE HEAVYWEIGHT CHAMPION OF THE INTERNET"

If net neutrality were a boxing match, in one corner would be the combined strength of AT&T, Comcast, Verizon, and TimeWarner. In the other corner you'd find the amalgamated power of the likes of Amazon, Netflix, Facebook, eBay, Microsoft, and Google.

Back in 2007, candidate Barack Obama made clear his opinion on net neutrality by pledging his support "to protect a free and open Internet if elected President." He went on to say, "I am a strong supporter of net neutrality." And then he added, "What you've been seeing is some lobbying that says that servers and the various portals through which you're getting information over the Internet should be able to be gatekeepers and to charge different rates to different websites. . . . And that I think destroys one of the best things about the Internet—which is that there is this incredible equality there."

Behemoths AT&T etc. didn't quite agree. *Business Insider* noted: "Over time, companies like Comcast have gotten tired of serving bandwidth hogs like Netflix (that often accounts for up to 50 percent of streaming at any one time), and paying for the privilege of doing so. . . . AT&T has been even more blunt. Netflix has built a business that requires a huge amount of bandwidth, but it doesn't want to pay for it."

Comcast and Netflix reached a deal that basically said Netflix would pay Comcast for a direct connection between its servers and Comcast's so that Netflix's traffic didn't have to go through the interconnect companies. But Netflix and others still maintained that prices should be the same for all.

That led to a May 2010 action by the Federal Communications Commission (FCC) that said Internet service providers could not block websites or impose limits on users. The final version, passed in December of that year, was intended to prevent broadband Internet service providers from blocking or interfering with traffic on the Web. In other words, everything remained a level playing field.

Weeks after the FCC adopted their rules, Verizon Communications filed a federal lawsuit aimed at overturning the order.

By 2013 the DC Circuit Court was hearing arguments in opposition to the FCC's Open Internet Order, which created that first form of net neutrality in 2010. The issues were complicated, but they included arguments about whether the FCC had the right to regulate the Internet at all.

In January 2014, a Federal appeals court struck down the 2010 FCC rule. And one day later, a user created a petition on the White House's "We the People" platform urging the Obama administration to "Restore Net Neutrality by Directing the FCC to Classify Internet Providers as 'Common Carriers.'" This move opposed the providers' keeping their classification as providers of "information services," which they had been since Congress passed the 1996 Telecommunications Act.

The White House made it clear at the time that it supported a free and open Internet, simultaneously saying it couldn't direct an independent agency's rule-making activity.

In May 2014, FCC chairman Tom Wheeler, who had been appointed by President Obama on November 4, 2013, released a plan that would have allowed AT&T etc. to discriminate online and create pay-to-play fast lanes. He also invited the public to weigh in on the subject.

Not only did millions protest, but Amazon etc. (including Google) aligned themselves with the so-called "little guy." Net neutrality became "crucial for small business owners, startups and entrepreneurs" that needed the Internet to launch their businesses, create a market, and advertise. In essence, the Internet made it possible for anyone and everyone to start a business. Thus AT&T etc. were gatekeepers to the Internet. Without net neutrality, "they would seize every possible opportunity to profit from that gatekeeper control."

A "Dear FCC Commissioners" letter was sent on May 7, 2014:

> We write to express our support for a free and open Internet. Over the past twenty years, American innovators have created countless Internet-based applications, content offerings, and services that are used around the world. These inno-

vations have created enormous value for Internet users, fueled economic growth, and made our Internet companies global leaders. The innovation we have seen to date happened in a world without discrimination. An open Internet has also been a platform for free speech and opportunity for billions of users.

The Commission's long-standing commitment and actions undertaken to protect the open Internet are a central reason why the Internet remains an engine of entrepreneurship and economic growth.

According to recent news reports, the Commission intends to propose rules that would enable phone and cable Internet service providers to discriminate both technically and financially against Internet companies and to impose new tolls on them. If these reports are correct, this represents a grave threat to the Internet. . . .

The rules should provide certainty to all market participants and keep the costs of regulation low. Such rules are essential for the future of the Internet. This Commission should take the necessary steps to ensure that the Internet remains an open platform for speech and commerce so that America continues to lead the world in technology markets.

It was signed by Amazon etc.'s entire corner—including Google and many, many friends.

The president gave his opinion in August 2014, backing up the position of Amazon etc. and even mentioning some of the members specifically: "I personally, the position of my administration, as well as a lot of companies here, is that you don't want to start getting a differentiation in how accessible the Internet is to different users. You want to leave it open so the next Google and the next Facebook can succeed."

One month later, the *Washington Post* ran a headline: "Google's studied silence on net neutrality has finally broken." The article said:

After a long silence, one of the Internet's biggest companies has finally weighed in on the latest net neutrality debate.

On Wednesday, Google said it would oppose efforts by

large Internet providers to speed up, slow down or manipulate Internet traffic that their customers request. Although Google has recently spoken out on net neutrality through industry groups and think tanks, this marks the first time since 2010 that Google has staked out an explicit position of its own on the policy.

"If Internet access providers can block some services and cut special deals that prioritize some companies' content over others, that would threaten the innovation that makes the Internet awesome," wrote Google in a message to Internet activists Wednesday. "No Internet access provider should block or degrade Internet traffic, nor should they sell 'fast lanes' that prioritize particular Internet services over others."

While Google stopped short of endorsing a particular policy prescription—some Internet activists, for example, are calling for the Federal Communications Commission to begin regulating broadband providers under a part of the communications law known as Title II; others argue such a step isn't needed—the company's strongly worded statement envisions a far-reaching policy that would touch not only providers of fixed broadband like cable companies, but also wireless carriers.

Title II is a section of the Communications Act of 1934 that deals with common carriers. The Roosevelt Institute provides the following description:

> Written and passed during FDR's first term, the Communications Act of 1934 consolidated existing radio, television, and telephone regulations and created the Federal Communications Commission (FCC) to oversee all interstate and foreign communications. It was intended to streamline the regulatory process and expand affordable access to communication services.
>
> As communications networks came to occupy a more prominent role in American society, the FCC's influence grew along with them. Throughout its history, it has often provoked controversy due to its efforts to police obscene content, which

some see as a violation of free speech. In 1996, the Telecommunications Act amended the 1934 law in an attempt to bring it up to date with modern technology. However, critics noted that the new law also weakened ownership rules designed to prevent the growth of telecom monopolies.

Currently the FCC is at the center of the debate over net neutrality. In 2002, it ruled that most forms of broadband Internet access did not qualify as telecommunications services, and were therefore not subject to Title II's common carrier regulations. Supporters of net neutrality, who believe that the Internet must be kept free and equally accessible to everyone, argue that the FCC should establish new regulations to include broadband Internet services or that Congress should pass another law to expand the FCC's authority.

As input continued, President Obama, in a video announcement on November 14, 2014, reiterated his support for strong, open Internet rules and for the first time explicitly called for those rules to be grounded in Title II authority. He said, "Ever since the Internet was created it's been organized around the principles of openness, fairness and freedom. There are no gatekeepers deciding which sites you get to access."

As stated before, you have to remove your political allegiances and make sure you have your Newsvesting lenses in place. Politics may make strange bedfellows, but profits take them to a whole new level.

On February 4, 2015, FCC chairman Tom Wheeler endorsed strong, open Internet rules grounded in Title II authority. He said:

> Originally, I believed that the FCC could assure internet openness through a determination of "commercial reasonableness" under Section 706 of the Telecommunications Act of 1996. While a recent court decision seemed to draw a roadmap for using this approach, I became concerned that this relatively new concept might, down the road, be interpreted to mean what is reasonable for commercial interests, not consumers.
>
> That is why I am proposing that the FCC use its Title II authority to implement and enforce open internet protections.

> Using this authority, I am submitting to my colleagues
> the strongest open internet protections ever proposed by
> the FCC. These enforceable, bright-line rules will ban paid
> prioritization, and the blocking and throttling of lawful con-
> tent and services. I propose to fully apply—for the first time
> ever—those bright-line rules to mobile broadband.

In a three-to-two party-line vote on February 26, 2015, the FCC passed open Internet rules applying to both wired and wireless Internet connections grounded in Title II authority.

The *New York Times* reported on March 12, 2015, that the FCC's release of the rules "revealed how the strict laws would be modified for Internet providers, exempting the companies from the sort of price controls typically applied to utilities, for example. But the full text of the new order also raised uncertainties about broad and subjective regulations. One catchall provision, requiring 'just and reasonable' conduct, allows the F.C.C. to decide what is acceptable on a case-by-case basis."

A *Human Events* article delved into the topic with and article titled "Who wins with Obama's net neutrality?" Get ready—this is where Newsvestors might have to put on some political blinders. *Human Events* said:

> Then there are the giant Friends of Obama companies
> who will benefit tremendously from this—first among them
> Netflix and Google. These two companies alone consume
> more than half of all U.S. web traffic. And the Administration's
> grab just outlawed their being charged for it.
>
> Internet Service Providers (ISPs) can only charge two peo-
> ple for the bandwidth they build. Hogs like Netflix and
> Google—or us. So our prices will skyrocket—to augment the
> profits of Hogs like Netflix and Google.

The article goes on to suggest that chairman Wheeler tweaked the net neutrality plan after a "Google push."

> The Obama Administration wouldn't take input from Con-
> gress or Republicans on the Commission. They wouldn't let
> We the People read it. But somehow Google got a copy, didn't

like part of it—and FCC head-waiter Wheeler dutifully took their order.

What was the upshot of the FCC ruling? That remains to be seen. But as *Digital Trends* quoted a Fox News report in April 2015:

> When it comes to the heated debate over Net neutrality, Google is putting on the white hat, and painting itself as the hero of the story. The company recently released a blog post regarding the expansion of its lightning-fast Google Fiber service, implicitly promising that the service will be the champion of streaming services like Netflix. So who's the subtly implied villain in the tale? Comcast, of course, the company currently under fire for its "pay-for-speed" deal with Netflix, among other things.
>
> Internet service providers, the ones that show up on your monthly bill, generally don't have a lot to do with the vast majority of the long journey your video packets make from servers, such as those in Netflix's own facilities, across the thousands of miles of plains, mountains, and valleys to end up at your TV. Those providers mostly deal with what's called the "last mile," or the direct link from the Web's pipelines into those connected to your home. . . .
>
> Google has promised to freely offer high-bandwidth content providers. The story, as you might expect, is much more complicated than all that. But the basic gist of Google's message is the promise that its new Fiber service, which will directly compete with Internet service providers like Comcast and Verizon, will not charge content providers. . . . Instead, it will offer those partnerships completely free of charge.
>
> Thanks to all that attention, with Fiber, Google is able do a lot of things that may be good for innovation online, but are also very good for Google.

Whether it's a net neutrality victory, new products, new algorithms, or the package in total, Google can seemingly do no wrong. In April 2015, a

Forbes report gave the following news about what would usually be seen as a dismal first-quarter earnings report:

> Google's reported first-quarter financials came up shy of expectations across the board, missing on quarterly revenue, earnings, paid clicks and cost-per-click. . . . Paid clicks grew 13%, down from 14% a quarter ago. Cost-per-click, the amount marketers pay every time a user clicks on one of their ads, took a 13% dive, continuing a decline that began several quarters ago.
>
> Google's search business is under more scrutiny than usual following a showdown with the EU last week in which the commission accused Google of promoting its own shopping search results over its competitors', abusing its market leader position.

The response to all this foreboding news? Again citing *Forbes*, "Investors appeared to shrug off the weakness, sending shares up about 2.5% percent in after hours trading." Google shares traded at $540 at 9:30 a.m. on the day earnings were announced. At 9:30 a.m. the next day, they were up to $566. Perhaps they realized what good times were waiting right around the corner.

Friends in high places can come in handy. Especially when those friendships play out in public. Savvy Newsvestors not only recognize those relationships but also realize what they can mean to their investment opportunities. Yes, it can often mean using your head instead of your heart, but if realities interfere with principles, it's best to use the news to your advantage and count your Newsvestor profits while you live to fight another day politically. Administrations and friends of administrations come and go. There will always be a winner and a loser in any political race. But being on the short end of the vote doesn't mean you have to be on the short end of financial gain. Blue states and red states are one thing. In every state, the money is still green. When it comes to bipartisan business dealings, being a consistent Newsvestor is a good harbinger of success.

"THE MARKET TUMBLES" . . . AND NEWSVESTORS WERE READY

Remember that Opinion Savvy analysis of the Michigan Consumer Sentiment Index which I discussed in my syndicated column in April of 2015?

As it turns out, their analysis of that very important public opinion survey was indeed correct. Within four months of the publication of my Creators column, which ran on news and opinion sites such as Newsmax, Townhall, and in some daily newspapers, the market had taken a dive . . . a big dive.

The analysis of the sentiment survey in April suggested that the Michigan Index had reached levels of positive consumer sentiment that served as warning signs that things really were "too good to be true." The index had reached a level that strongly suggested the economy was perhaps not as strong as experts believed it to be and the long bull run in the market would face significant problems not too many months down the road.

The analysis was right, confirming once again that Newsvestors should keep a keen eye on public opinion and consumer sentiment surveys. On August 21, 2015, the Drudge Report, in typical Drudge style, reported the slide of the Dow industrials of more than 1000 points in five days with the blunt headline "BAM! BOOM GOES BUST." Between the release of my syndicated column focusing on the Opinion Savvy warning over it analysis of the Michigan Index in late April 2015, through most of July and into early August, the markets had bumped along. A chart of the Dow for that period looked like a typical EKG, rising a bit, then falling a bit, then rising again. But starting on Monday, August 17, and through the entire week that EKG-like chart took a nosedive.

When the decline in the stock market hit, it came quickly. Following the weeklong plummet the *Wall Street Journal* reported, "U.S. stocks suffered their worst losses in four years . . . (pushing stocks) into what money managers call a correction."

For Newsvestors who had pocketed profits while Newsvesting in the prior year, there was immediate reward and potential additional opportunity. Of course the reward was that by having moved to a greater cash position, Newsvestors held the value of their overall portfolio at a higher level than those who were more heavily invested in the market.

The opportunity was obvious. As the markets fell there was the chance to buy shares in good companies. Companies that ultimately would survive any major decline in the value of their shares and would ultimately grow in the next surge on Wall Street.

When that opportunity would come and how long it would be sustainable was the challenge for Newsvestors. With China's economy slowing substantially, Europe in economic trouble, Japan faltering, and oil prices plunging, it would take the discipline and methods of Newsvesting to navigate the financial waters. But armed with the tools of news and opinion, there could be little doubt that great opportunities were being presented for Newsvestors, even as the financial shape of the U.S. economy and its markets were very much up in the air going into the 2016 presidential contest.